# Baking with Vegetables

# Baking *with* Vegetables

ADD KALE TO YOUR CAKE AND FEEL
VIRTUOUS WHILE YOU BAKE

This edition published by Parragon Books Ltd in 2015
and distributed by

Parragon Inc.
440 Park Avenue South, 13th Floor
New York, NY 10016
www.parragon.com/lovefood

ISBN 978-1-4723-8988-6

Printed in China

New recipes and text written by Christine McFadden
New photography by Haarala Hamilton
Edited by Fiona Biggs

Notes for the Reader
This book uses standard kitchen measuring spoons and cups. All spoon and cup measurements are level
unless otherwise indicated. Unless otherwise stated, milk is assumed to be whole, eggs are large,
individual vegetables are medium, and pepper is freshly ground black pepper. Unless otherwise stated,
all root vegetables should be peeled prior to using.

The times given are only an approximate guide. Preparation times differ according to the techniques
used by different people and the cooking times may also vary from those given.

Using vegetables in cakes and baked desserts isn't new. Carrot cake and pumpkin pie are long-time American favorites, and on Italy's Amalfi coast a sweet concoction of eggplant and chocolate is a must-have summer dessert. The Swiss and Germans are partial to mashed potato-and-chocolate cakes, and in the Middle East carrot cakes and desserts are traditional. In Great Britain, a 2011 survey established carrot cake as the nation's favorite cake. If carrots, pumpkins, and potatoes work well, there's no reason why other vegetables can't be given the same treatment. How about cauliflower or parsnips? If you enjoy baking, the possibilities are as exciting as they are intriguing. Given that the word "vegetable" comes from the Latin verb vegere, meaning "to enliven," it's hardly surprising that vegetable cakes are so successful. They're fun to make, and the vegetables add color and improve texture. If you grow your own, using them in baked goods is a great way of dealing with seasonal bumper crops.

## Upping Your Intake

Vegetables are good for you. A 12-year study undertaken by University College London claims that to reduce the risk of heart disease, stroke, diabetes, and obesity, we should be eating seven or more portions of vegetables and fruit a day—and these should be mostly vegetables. The United States Department of Agriculture (USDA) advice for adults is to consume 2-3 cups daily of raw or cooked vegetables (but 2 cups of raw leafy greens equals 1 cup), depending on age, gender, and calorie intake—or about half your plate. In Great Britain the advice is "five a day" and in Australia it's five portions of vegetables and two of fruit.

## Vegetables vs. Fruit

From a health point of view, vegetables win hands down over fruit. They deliver a far greater range of important nutrients—for example, iron, calcium, and folate—plus more dietary fiber. Vegetables contain far less sugar than fruit—even "sweet" vegetables, such as corn, bell peppers, and sweet potatoes, contain significantly less sugar than fruit. Levels of vitamin C and potassium in fruit and vegetables are about the same, but when it comes to vitamin A (vital for children's growth, normal vision, and healthy skin and membranes), dark, leafy greens and orange-flesh vegetables outstrip apricots, melons, and mangoes. Fruit is more acidic than vegetables, so more sugar has to be added, and the high juice content can make cakes heavy.

## Why Not Vegetables?

Using vegetables as a core ingredient makes cakes and desserts less of a guilt-ridden indulgence.

Root vegetables—for example, carrots, parsnips, and beets—are baking stars. They are naturally slightly sweet—so you can cut down on added sugar—they are rich in dietary fiber, and, like all vegetables, they provide all-important moisture. This improves the texture of your cakes and, better yet, means you can scale back the fat.

You can use vegetables to make food colorings. Just blend them in a blender and use the juice to tint icing, frosting, buttercream, or marzipan. Small leaves and feathery leaves make attractive decorations, too.

## Successful Sourcing

Successful baked goods rely on top-quality
ingredients. Knowing the best places to buy
vegetables is important, or if you grow your
own, when the best time is to harvest them.
Where you buy vegetables depends on how
much time you have, how far you can travel,
whether or not you prefer to support the local
economy, and how concerned you are about where
they come from.

**FARM STORES**—The best farm stores grow their
own vegetables and harvest on a daily basis.
The produce is not necessarily inexpensive,
but it is usually of high quality, seasonal,
and especially fresh.

**FARMERS' MARKETS**—Vegetables are locally
grown and the grower will probably be there
to tell you more about the varieties and how
they have been grown.

**COMMUNITY SUPPORTED AGRICULTURE (CSA)**—
Becoming a member of a CSA partnership means
that seasonal vegetables are delivered to
your door on a regular basis and you'll
be supporting local farms. Be prepared
for surprises and repetition. Baking with
vegetables will enable you to use up any odds
and ends that are left in your box.

**RETAIL GROCERY STORES**—Whole-food stores and
gourmet food stores often stock high-quality
vegetables, including vegetables that may be
hard to find in supermarkets. Local grocery
stores can be a good source of fresh seasonal
vegetables. Always inspect the vegetables
before you buy.

**SUPERMARKETS**—They provide an enormous choice
of fresh produce, some of which is packaged
after being prepared. Vegetables are often
imported, with means there is greater year-
round availability.

*Remember to wash all
fresh vegetables before
using them, even those
that are packaged and
labeled as prewashed.*

## When to Buy

Climate varies from country to country and
region to region, and, with the effect of
global warming, the weather is becoming more
unpredictable. This means that the season
for certain vegetables—for example, peas and
pumpkins—may be shorter or longer, or earlier
or later than you might expect.

   If you don't subscribe to a CSA membership,
keep an eye on what's for sale at your local
farm store, farmer's market, or grocery store.

## What to Buy

Although flavor depends on variety and the
skill of the grower, it's worth keeping in
mind that harvesting vegetables at their peak
of ripeness for immediate sale also plays an
important part.

**ORGANIC VEGETABLES**—These have not been
doused with pesticides and artificial
fertilizers, nor have they been genetically
modified. In taste tests, they consistently
do much better than intensively farmed
vegetables. Organic carrots and red bell
peppers are particularly full of flavor.

**LOCALLY GROWN VEGETABLES**—They may not be
organic but are often grown using minimal
amounts of chemicals and will probably be
just as delicious as those that have been
grown organically.

**HEIRLOOM VARIETIES**—These have been grown by
generations of farmers and gardeners and are
valued for their wonderful flavor.

**PICK-YOUR-OWN FARMS**—These usually have
varieties that are known to do well in a
particular region.

# Essential Baking Equipment

Baking is a simple pleasure and many recipes require minimal equipment to achieve beautiful results. However, not having the right equipment on hand can be the undoing of even the most experienced baker. Make sure you read the recipe carefully before you start to ensure that you have everything you need close at hand while you work.

### MEASURING CUPS
A set of measuring cups is essential for accurately measuring ingredients and they hold the key to successful baking. Use the back edge of a blunt knife to level off dry ingredients. A large heatproof glass measuring cup will also be useful for measuring liquids.

### MEASURING SPOONS
These are useful for accurately measuring small quantities of ingredients, such as leavening agents, ground spices, and extracts.

### WOODEN SPOONS
Larger wooden spoons are essential for creaming, mixing, and stirring, so it's good to have a few of these in varying sizes.

### SPATULAS
A good rubber or silicone spatula will enable you to scrape out as much dough or batter as possible and transfer it to your baking pan or sheet.

### MIXING BOWLS
Two or three mixing bowls in different sizes are useful. Heatproof glass bowls are durable and practical, and melamine or ceramic bowls come in assorted bright colors.

### PAPER CUPCAKE LINERS & MUFFIN CUPS
Paper cupcake liners and muffin cups are widely available in supermarkets, kitchenware stores, and online in many bright colors and patterns, and several sizes. Silicone cups are available in a range of colors and sizes and make good reusable alternatives.

### BAKING SHEETS & PANS
Metal baking sheets and pans, both standard and nonstick, are invaluable for baking cookies and other sweet treats. Baking pans come in a wide range of shapes and sizes, including deep or shallow round and square cake pans, loaf pans, brownie pans, cupcake and muffin pans, loose-bottom tart pans, plus individual or mini pans. Silicone bakeware is available in all shapes and sizes, reducing the need for lining and greasing.

### ELECTRIC HANDHELD MIXERS & STAND MIXERS
An electric mixer makes light work of mixing or beating mixtures such as cake batters. Handheld mixers are easy to use, and a freestanding stand mixer can be used for many tasks.

### PASTRY BAGS & TIPS
Pastry bags and a small selection of tips are essential for adding that special finishing flourish to cakes and desserts. Strong nylon or fabric bags are washable and reusable, while disposable plastic or paper bags save work. A few stainless-steel or plastic pastry tips are the key to perfect piping. A basic set of tips should include a plain writing tip, a large plain tip, and small and large star tips.

# CHAPTER 1:

## Cakes, Small Bites & Breads

# Zucchini Loaf Cake with Cream Cheese Frosting

*Zucchini cake is one of the big surprises in the home baker's repertoire. It's a great way to use up a bumper crop of zucchini, and it is just as moist and delicious as its well-known cousin, the carrot cake.*

## SERVES 10

### Ingredients

1¾ CUPS GROUND ALMONDS
  (ALMOND MEAL)
½ TEASPOON BAKING POWDER
½ TEASPOON BAKING SODA
3 TABLESPOONS STEVIA
⅓ CUP CHOPPED MIXED NUTS
2 TABLESPOONS BUTTER
2 EXTRA-LARGE EGGS, BEATEN
1 TEASPOON VANILLA EXTRACT
2 CUPS SHREDDED ZUCCHINI

### Frosting

1 CUP CREAM CHEESE
1 TABLESPOON STEVIA
FINELY GRATED ZEST AND JUICE
  OF ¼ UNWAXED LEMON

1. Preheat the oven to 325°F. Line a nonstick loaf pan with parchment paper.

2. Put the ground almonds, baking powder, baking soda, stevia, and half the nuts into a large bowl and stir well.

3. Melt the butter in a small saucepan over medium-low heat. Pour it onto the dry ingredients. Add the eggs, vanilla extract, and zucchini and mix well.

4. Spoon the batter into the prepared pan and spread it in an even layer. Bake for 55-60 minutes, or until well risen and a toothpick inserted into the center of the cake comes out clean. Let cool in the pan for 15 minutes, then remove from the pan, peel off the parchment paper, and transfer to a wire rack to cool completely.

5. To make the frosting, put the cream cheese and stevia into a large bowl and beat until light and airy. Add the lemon zest and juice, and beat again briefly. Using a spatula, spread the frosting over the top of the cake. Decorate with the remaining nuts and serve.

...

## Cook's Tip

*If you intend to use the zest, try to buy unwaxed lemons. If you can't find any, scrub waxed lemons well before use. Lemons should always be firm and heavy, with a thick, knobbly skin and no green tinges.*

# Spiced Squash Cake

Squash adds a rich texture and depth to sweet cakes and it is a perfect complement to dried fruit and warming spices. This deliciously moist cake would be the perfect choice for a Halloween party.

---

## SERVES 8

### Ingredients

⅓ CUP GOLDEN RAISINS
1¼ STICKS UNSALTED BUTTER, PLUS
  ½ TABLESPOON FOR GREASING
3 CUPS PEELED, SEEDED, AND
  DICED BUTTERNUT SQUASH
  (ABOUT ½ LARGE SQUASH)
¾ CUP SUPERFINE SUGAR
½ CUP CHOPPED ALMONDS
¼ CUP ITALIAN CANDIED PEEL
FINELY GRATED ZEST OF 1 LEMON

1½ TEASPOONS GROUND CINNAMON
1½ TEASPOONS GROUND GINGER
¾ CUP KAMUT FLOUR
1 HEAPING TEASPOON BAKING
  POWDER
2 EGGS, SEPARATED
1 TABLESPOON CONFECTIONERS'
  SUGAR, FOR DUSTING

---

1. Put the golden raisins into a bowl, pour enough boiling water over them to cover, and let soak.

2. Preheat the oven to 350°F. Grease and line a 9-inch round springform cake pan.

3. Put the squash and butter into a saucepan. Cover and cook over medium heat for about 15 minutes, until soft. Transfer to a bowl and beat until smooth.

4. Stir in the sugar, almonds, candied peel, lemon zest, cinnamon, ginger, and golden raisins, and mix well to combine.

5. Sift together the flour and baking powder, tipping in any bran remaining in the sifter. Gradually beat into the squash mixture.

6. Beat the egg yolks for about 3 minutes, until thick. Fold into the squash mixture.

7. Whisk the egg whites until they hold stiff peaks. Fold carefully into the mixture, using a large metal spoon. Spoon the batter into the prepared pan.

8. Bake in the preheated oven for 1 hour, or until a toothpick inserted into the center comes out clean. Turn out onto a wire rack to cool. Dust with the confectioners' sugar just before serving.

...

## Cook's Tip

*Finely peeled curls of lemon or orange zest sprinkled over the top of the cake would make a pretty decoration for a special occasion.*

# Spinach & Apple Cake with Apple Frosting

Crisp, grated apple and a tangy, unsweetened applesauce add texture and fresh flavor to this unusual green cake. The cake is a favorite in Turkey, where cooks use the colorful crumbs as a decoration for the frosting.

## Cook's Tip

When preparing the spinach, make sure that you squeeze out as much water as possible before pureeing. Cooked spinach holds a lot of water, and any excess liquid will have an adverse impact on the texture of the finished cake.

14

**SERVES 12**

*Ingredients*

½ CUP CANOLA OIL, PLUS
  1 TABLESPOON FOR OILING
3 (6-OUNCE) PACKAGES BABY
  SPINACH (ABOUT 18 CUPS)
2¼ CUPS SPELT FLOUR
1 TABLESPOON BAKING POWDER
½ TEASPOON SALT
3 EGGS
¾ CUP SUPERFINE SUGAR
3 TABLESPOONS LEMON JUICE

1 SMALL CRISP SWEET APPLE, SUCH
  AS PIPPIN, COARSELY GRATED
2 TEASPOONS VANILLA EXTRACT

*Frosting*

2 COOKING APPLES, SUCH AS
  GRANNY SMITH, CUT INTO
  LARGE CHUNKS
1¾ CUPS CONFECTIONERS' SUGAR,
  SIFTED
2 TABLESPOONS BUTTER, SOFTENED
½ TEASPOON FINELY GRATED
  LEMON PEEL

1. Preheat the oven to 350°F. Oil an 8½-inch square cake pan and line with parchment paper.

2. Steam the spinach for 3 minutes, squeeze dry, transfer to a blender, and puree until smooth. Set aside until needed.

3. Sift the flour, baking powder, and salt twice into a bowl. Put the eggs and sugar into a separate large bowl and beat with a handheld electric mixer for 5 minutes, or until pale and creamy. Lightly beat in the oil, lemon juice, apple, vanilla extract and spinach puree. Gradually stir in the flour mixture.

4. Pour the batter into the prepared pan. Bake in the preheated oven for 25-30 minutes, until a toothpick inserted into the center comes out clean. Let cool in the pan for 10 minutes, then turn out onto a wire rack and let cool completely.

5. Using a sharp serrated knife, trim about ⅜ inch from all four sides of the cake. Scoop out the green part from underneath these crusts, rub into crumbs using your fingertips, and set aside.

6. To make the frosting, put the apples into a saucepan with a little water, bring to a simmer over medium-low heat, and cook until soft. Mash with a fork, then push through a strainer into a bowl. Add the remaining ingredients and mix well. Spoon over the top of the cake and sprinkle with a few of the reserved green crumbs. Slice into squares to serve.

...

# Carrot Cake

It's amazing that shredded carrot incorporated into a cake recipe can taste so delicious. Maybe it's the luxurious cream cheese frosting spread generously over the top that tips the balance in its favor.

SERVES 12

## Ingredients

½ TABLESPOON BUTTER, FOR
 GREASING
¾ CUP ALL-PURPOSE FLOUR
¾ TEASPOON BAKING POWDER
PINCH OF SALT
1 TEASPOON GROUND ALLSPICE
½ TEASPOON GROUND NUTMEG
½ CUP FIRMLY PACKED LIGHT
 BROWN SUGAR
2 EGGS, BEATEN
⅓ CUP SUNFLOWER OIL

2 CARROTS, SHREDDED
1 BANANA, CHOPPED
¼ CUP CHOPPED MIXED NUTS,
 TOASTED
24 WALNUT HALVES, TO DECORATE

## Frosting

3 TABLESPOONS BUTTER, SOFTENED
3 TABLESPOONS CREAM CHEESE
1⅓ CUPS CONFECTIONERS' SUGAR,
 SIFTED
1 TEASPOON FRESH ORANGE JUICE
GRATED ZEST OF ½ ORANGE

1. Preheat the oven to 350°F. Grease a 7-inch square cake pan and line with parchment paper.

2. Sift the flour, baking powder, salt, allspice, and nutmeg into a bowl. Stir in the brown sugar, then stir in the eggs and oil. Add the carrots, banana, and mixed nuts and mix well to combine.

3. Spoon the batter into the prepared pan and level the surface. Bake in the preheated oven for 35-40 minutes, or until golden and just firm to the touch. Let cool slightly. When the cake is cool enough to handle, turn out onto a wire rack and let cool completely.

4. For the frosting, put the butter, cream cheese, confectioners' sugar, orange juice, and zest into a bowl and beat together until creamy. Spread the frosting over the top of the cold cake, then use a fork to make shallow, wavy lines. Cut into squares, decorate each with walnut halves, and serve.

...

## Variation

For a less formal finish to these squares, you could sprinkle a few chopped walnuts over the frosting.

# Pea & Lemon Verbena Cake with Lemon Icing

*Young peas paired with fragrant lemon verbena make a superb light and delicious summery cake. Lemon verbena syrup and refreshing lemon icing enhance the citrus flavor.*

## SERVES 12

### Ingredients

1¾ STICKS UNSALTED BUTTER,
  AT ROOM TEMPERATURE, PLUS
  ½ TABLESPOON BUTTER, FOR
  GREASING
1¾ CUPS FRESH OR FROZEN PEAS
2 CUPS SPELT FLOUR
1 TABLESPOON BAKING POWDER
¼ TEASPOON SALT

¾ CUP SUPERFINE SUGAR
3 TABLESPOONS FINELY CHOPPED
  FRESH LEMON VERBENA
3 EGGS

### Syrup

⅓ CUP SUPERFINE SUGAR
8 FRESH LEMON VERBENA SPRIGS
⅓ CUP WATER

### Icing

2⅔ CUPS CONFECTIONERS' SUGAR,
  SIFTED
5-6 TABLESPOONS LEMON JUICE
2-3 DROPS GREEN FOOD COLORING

---

1. Grease an 8-inch square cake pan and line with parchment paper. Preheat the oven to 325°F.

2. Bring a small saucepan of water to a boil. Add the peas, bring back to a boil, and cook for 3 minutes, until just tender. Drain and refresh under cold running water. Puree in a food processor for 2-3 minutes, until smooth, frequently scraping down the sides of the bowl.

3. Sift the flour, baking powder, and salt twice into a mixing bowl.

4. Using a mortar and pestle, grind 3 tablespoons of the sugar with the lemon verbena. Put the butter, remaining sugar, and lemon verbena mixture into a bowl and beat with a handheld electric mixer for 3 minutes, until light and fluffy. Add the eggs, one at a time, alternating with the flour mixture and beating well after each addition. Stir in the pea puree, mixing well with a fork.

5. Spoon the batter into the prepared pan, leveling the surface. Bake in the preheated oven for 25-30 minutes, turning halfway through, or until a toothpick inserted into the center comes out clean. Let cool in the pan for 10 minutes, then turn out onto a wire rack with the bottom of the cake facing upward and let cool completely.

6. To make the syrup, put all the ingredients into a small saucepan. Bring to a boil and simmer for 1 minute. Remove from the heat and set aside. Set the cake, still on the rack, over a pan. Drain the syrup, then spoon it over the cake and let soak in.

7. To make the icing, mix the confectioners' sugar with the lemon juice, adding 1 tablespoon of juice at a time, until you have a smooth coating consistency. Pour all but 1 cup of the icing over the cake, allowing it to spread down the sides.

8. Add a few drops of food coloring to the reserved icing. Decant into a pastry bag fitted with a small plain tip. Pipe sprigs and small round mounds over the cake to resemble lemon verbena leaves and peas.

. . .

# Beet & Coconut Chocolate Cake

**SERVES 10-12**

## Ingredients

5 BEETS (ABOUT 1 POUND), TRIMMED
½ TABLESPOON BUTTER, FOR
  GREASING
1¾ CUPS SPELT FLOUR
½ CUP UNSWEETENED COCOA POWDER
2 TEASPOONS BAKING POWDER
1 CUP SUPERFINE SUGAR
4 OUNCES BITTERSWEET CHOCOLATE,
  BROKEN INTO SMALL PIECES
3 EGGS
1 CUP SOLID COCONUT OIL

## Chocolate Glaze

3 TABLESPOONS SUPERFINE SUGAR
3 TABLESPOONS MILK
3 OUNCES SEMISWEET CHOCOLATE,
  BROKEN INTO SMALL PIECES
6 TABLESPOONS UNSALTED BUTTER

## Beet Icing

2-2½ TABLESPOONS WATER
1 CUP CONFECTIONERS' SUGAR,
  SIFTED
1 TEASPOON BEET POWDER

1. Peel the beets, slice into ½-inch chunks, and steam for 30 minutes, until tender. Alternatively, microwave on High for 10 minutes. Puree for 2-3 minutes in a mini-food processor, frequently scraping down the sides of the bowl. Set aside until needed.

2. Preheat the oven to 325°F. Grease a 9-inch round springform cake pan and line it with parchment paper.

3. Sift the flour, cocoa powder, and baking powder twice into a bowl. Mix in the sugar.

4. Put the chocolate into a heatproof bowl set over a saucepan of gently simmering water and heat until melted.

5. Put the beet puree into the bowl of a food processor. With the machine running, add the eggs, one at a time, then add the oil. Stir the beet mixture into the dry ingredients, then add the melted chocolate.

6. Spoon the batter into the prepared pan. Bake in the preheated oven for 50-60 minutes or until a toothpick inserted into the center comes out clean. Cover with aluminum foil if the top starts to brown too quickly. Let the cake cool in the pan for 10 minutes, then turn out onto a wire rack and let cool completely.

7. To make the chocolate glaze, put the ingredients into a small saucepan and melt over medium-low heat, stirring constantly. Spoon the glaze over the cooled cake, letting it trickle down the sides.

8. To make the beet icing, gradually stir enough of the water into the confectioners' sugar to make a soft paste. Stir in the beet powder. Decant into a decorating syringe fitted with a small plain tip and pipe thin zigzags across the cake.

...

# Spiced Parsnip & Orange Cupcakes with Orange Drizzle

MAKES 12

## Ingredients

1¾ CUPS SPELT FLOUR
2 TEASPOONS BAKING POWDER
½ TEASPOON BAKING SODA
¼ TEASPOON SALT
1 TEASPOON CHINESE FIVE SPICE
2 PARSNIPS, FINELY GRATED
2 TABLESPOONS FINELY CHOPPED
  CRYSTALLIZED GINGER
1½ TABLESPOONS FINELY GRATED
  ORANGE ZEST
1 STICK UNSALTED BUTTER,
  AT ROOM TEMPERATURE
⅔ CUP SUPERFINE SUGAR
2 EGGS
¼ CUP ORANGE JUICE
⅔ CUP BUTTERMILK
SLIVERS OF CRYSTALLIZED GINGER,
  TO DECORATE (OPTIONAL)

## Orange Drizzle

¾ CUP CONFECTIONERS' SUGAR,
  SIFTED
1-2 TABLESPOONS ORANGE JUICE

1. Preheat the oven to 350°F. Line a 12-cup muffin pan with paper cupcake liners.

2. Sift the flour, baking powder, baking soda, salt, and five spice twice into a bowl. Stir in the parsnip, ginger, and orange zest, mixing well with a fork.

3. Put the butter and sugar into a bowl and beat with a handheld mixer for about 3 minutes, until light and fluffy. Beat in the eggs, one at a time, alternating with the flour mixture and beating well after each addition. Gradually beat in the orange juice and buttermilk.

4. Spoon the batter into the paper liners and bake in the preheated oven for 20-25 minutes, turning the pan halfway through the cooking time, until a toothpick inserted into the center of a cupcake comes out clean.

5. Let cool in the pan for 10 minutes, then transfer to a wire rack and let cool completely.

6. To make the orange drizzle, put the confectioners' sugar into a bowl. Stir in the orange juice, 1 teaspoon at a time, until the mixture is runny enough to pipe.

7. Decant the drizzle into a decorating syringe and pipe zigzags over the tops of the cakes. Decorate with a few slivers of crystallized ginger, if using.

...

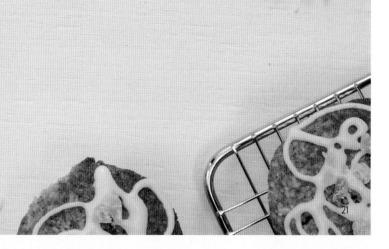

# Sweet Potato & Coconut Cupcakes with Lime & Coconut Frosting

*Bring a taste of the tropics to your table with these wonderful coconut- and lime-flavored cupcakes. Similar to squash, orange-fleshed sweet potato creates a beautiful color and moist texture.*

## MAKES 16-18

### Ingredients

2 SWEET POTATOES
1½ CUPS SPELT FLOUR
2 TEASPOONS BAKING POWDER
½ TEASPOON BAKING SODA
½ TEASPOON GROUND GINGER
¼ TEASPOON SALT
¾ CUP SUPERFINE SUGAR
½ CUP SOLID COCONUT OIL
2 EXTRA-LARGE EGGS

### Frosting

2 STICKS UNSALTED BUTTER
AT ROOM TEMPERATURE, DICED
2⅔ CUPS CONFECTIONERS' SUGAR,
SIFTED
⅓ CUP COCONUT CREAM (SCOOPED
FROM A CAN OF COCONUT MILK)
½ TEASPOON VANILLA EXTRACT
⅛ TEASPOON SALT
1½ TEASPOONS FINELY GRATED
LIME ZEST
1 TABLESPOON LIME JUICE

TOASTED COCONUT FLAKES,
TO DECORATE (OPTIONAL)
SLIVERS OF LIME ZEST,
TO DECORATE (OPTIONAL)

---

1. Preheat the oven to 425°F. Put the sweet potatoes into a baking pan and bake in the preheated oven for 45 minutes. Peel when cool enough to handle and puree in a food processor until smooth. Set aside until needed.

2. Reduce the oven temperature to 350°F. Line 16-18 cups in two muffin pans with paper cupcake liners.

3. Sift the flour, baking powder, baking soda, ginger, and salt twice into a bowl.

4. Put the sugar and oil into a separate bowl and beat with a handheld electric mixer for 3 minutes, until light and fluffy. Beat in the eggs, one at a time, alternating with the flour mixture and beating well after each addition. Stir in the sweet potato puree.

5. Spoon the batter into the paper liners, filling them about two-thirds full. Bake in the preheated oven for 15-20 minutes, turning the pans halfway through the cooking time, until a toothpick inserted into the center comes out clean. Let cool in the pan for 10 minutes, then transfer to a wire rack and let cool completely.

6. To make the frosting, put the butter and confectioners' sugar into a bowl and beat for 1 minute, or until fluffy. Beat in the remaining ingredients.

7. Swirl the frosting onto the cupcakes. Decorate with toasted coconut flakes and thin slivers of lime, if using.

...

## Cook's Tip

*Lift these luscious cupcakes out of the ordinary by adding some rum to the frosting mixture for an added kick.*

# Dark Chocolate, Black Pepper & Potato Mini Muffins

There's no better way to use up leftover mashed potatoes than in these irresistible dark chocolate muffins. A touch of black pepper adds bite to the muffin and a sprinkle of sugar adds a wonderful sparkle on top.

MAKES 12

*Ingredients*

1½ CUPS SPELT FLOUR

3 TABLESPOONS UNSWEETENED
COCOA POWDER

2 TEASPOONS BAKING POWDER

½ TEASPOON BAKING SODA

½ TEASPOON PEPPER

¼ TEASPOON SALT

⅓ CUP SUPERFINE SUGAR

1 STICK UNSALTED BUTTER,
AT ROOM TEMPERATURE

2 EGGS

1 CUP UNSEASONED COLD
MASHED POTATOES

½ CUP GREEK-STYLE YOGURT

2 TEASPOONS VANILLA EXTRACT

2 OUNCES BITTERSWEET CHOCOLATE,
CHOPPED INTO SMALL PIECES

1 TABLESPOON GRANULATED SUGAR
AND ¼ TEASPOON COARSELY GROUND
BLACK PEPPERCORNS, TO DECORATE

---

*1.* Preheat the oven to 350°F. Line a 12-cup muffin pan with paper muffin cups.

*2.* Sift the flour, cocoa powder, baking powder, baking soda, pepper, and salt twice into a bowl.

*3.* Put the sugar and butter into a bowl and beat with a handheld electric mixer for 2-3 minutes, until light and fluffy. Beat in the eggs, one at a time, alternating with the flour mixture. Stir in the potatoes, yogurt, vanilla extract, and chocolate.

*4.* Divide the batter among the paper cups in the prepared pan and bake in the preheated oven for 15-20 minutes, turning the pan halfway through the cooking time, until a toothpick inserted into the center of one of the muffins comes out clean.

*5.* Let cool in the pan for 10 minutes, then transfer to a wire rack and let cool completely.

*6.* While the muffins are still hot, combine the sugar with the ground peppercorns and sprinkle a little of the mixture over each cake.

...

# Red Cabbage & Apple
## Chocolate Muffins

These amazing muffins combine crisp apple, crunchy hazelnuts, and aromatic grated orange zest with shredded red cabbage. The cabbage is the secret to the moist texture, but you would never guess it is the main ingredient.

MAKES 12

## Ingredients

¾ CUP HAZELNUTS
1 TABLESPOON BUTTER, MELTED
1¼ CUPS ALL-PURPOSE FLOUR
1¼ CUPS WHOLE WHEAT FLOUR
¼ CUP UNSWEETENED COCOA POWDER
2 TEASPOONS BAKING POWDER
1 TEASPOON BAKING SODA
½ TEASPOON SALT
¼ TEASPOON FRESHLY GRATED NUTMEG
⅔ CUP GRANULATED SUGAR

1 TEASPOON LEMON JUICE
1⅛ CUPS SHREDDED RED CABBAGE,
 FINELY CHOPPED
½ CRISP SWEET APPLE, SUCH AS
 PIPPIN, GRATED
2 TEASPOONS FINELY GRATED
 ORANGE ZEST
2 EGGS
1 CUP BUTTERMILK
¼ CUP HAZELNUT OIL
2 TEASPOONS VANILLA EXTRACT

1. Preheat the oven to 350°F. Put the hazelnuts onto a baking sheet and toast in the preheated oven for 10 minutes. Rub off the skins, using a clean dish towel, coarsely chop, toss with the butter, and set aside.

2. Increase the oven temperature to 425°F. Line a 12-cup muffin pan with paper tulip-shape cups.

3. Sift together the all-purpose flour, whole wheat flour, cocoa powder, baking powder, baking soda, salt, and nutmeg into a large mixing bowl, tipping in any bran remaining in the sifter. Stir in the sugar.

4. Stir the lemon juice into the cabbage. Mix the cabbage, apple, and orange zest into the flour mixture, breaking up any clumps with your fingertips. Stir in the hazelnuts, mixing well.

5. Beat together the eggs, buttermilk, oil, and vanilla extract. Pour into the flour mixture, then stir until just combined. Do not overmix. Spoon about ¼ cup of the batter into each paper cup.

6. Bake for 15-20 minutes, or until a toothpick inserted into the center of a muffin comes out clean. Let cool in the pan for 10 minutes, then transfer to a wire rack to cool completely.

. . .

# Cauliflower Flatbreads

*These tasty flatbreads are stuffed with a spiced potato-and-cauliflower mixture. They are delicious eaten with yogurt or relishes, and can be served as an accompaniment to any main dish.*

MAKES 8

## Ingredients

1¾ CUPS WHOLE WHEAT FLOUR
¾ CUP ALL-PURPOSE FLOUR, PLUS
 1 TABLESPOON FOR DUSTING
1 TEASPOON FRESHLY GROUND
 CARDAMOM SEEDS
2 TEASPOONS SALT
1 CUP LUKEWARM BUTTERMILK
1¼ STICKS BUTTER, MELTED

## Filling

2 TABLESPOONS VEGETABLE OIL
2 TEASPOONS CUMIN SEEDS
1 TABLESPOON HOT CURRY POWDER
4 GARLIC CLOVES, CRUSHED
2 TEASPOONS FINELY GRATED
 FRESH GINGER
1 CUP FINELY CHOPPED
 CAULIFLOWER FLORETS
2 TEASPOONS SALT
2 POTATOES, BOILED, PEELED,
 AND COARSELY MASHED
⅓ CUP FINELY CHOPPED FRESH
 CILANTRO

1. To make the filling, heat the oil in a large skillet over medium heat. Add the cumin seeds, curry powder, garlic, ginger, and cauliflower and stir-fry for 8-10 minutes, or until the cauliflower is soft. Add the salt and the potatoes and stir well to mix evenly. Remove from the heat and stir in the cilantro. Let cool.

2. Sift together the whole wheat flour, all-purpose flour, cardamom seeds, and salt into a large bowl, tipping in any bran remaining in the sifter. Make a well in the center and pour in the buttermilk and 2 tablespoons of the melted butter. Work into the flour mixture to make a soft dough. Knead on a lightly floured surface for 10 minutes. Shape into a ball, put into a large bowl, cover with a damp cloth, and let rest for 20 minutes. Divide the dough into eight equal balls, then roll out each ball into a 6-inch disk.

3. Place a little of the filling in the center of each disk and fold up the edges of the dough into the center to enclose the filling. Press down lightly and roll out with a lightly floured rolling pin to a diameter of 6 inches. Repeat with the remaining dough and filling.

4. Heat a nonstick, flat, cast-iron griddle pan or heavy skillet over medium heat. Brush each flatbread with a little of the remaining melted butter. Brush the pan with a little melted butter. Put a flatbread on the pan and cook for 1-2 minutes, pressing down with a spatula. Turn over, brush with a little more butter, and cook for an additional 1-2 minutes, or until flecked with light brown spots. Remove from the pan, transfer to a plate, cover with aluminum foil, and keep warm while you cook the remaining flatbreads. Serve warm.

...

# Zucchini & Parmesan Bread

*The mustard and Parmesan cheese in this recipe add a zingy tang to an otherwise everyday loaf. It's delicious served with a hearty soup, or on its own fresh from the oven and spread with butter.*

MAKES 1 LOAF

## Ingredients

4 TABLESPOONS BUTTER, DICED,
 PLUS ½ TABLESPOON, FOR
 GREASING
1¾ CUPS ALL-PURPOSE FLOUR,
 PLUS 1 TABLESPOON FOR DUSTING
1¾ CUPS WHOLE WHEAT FLOUR
3½ TEASPOONS BAKING POWDER
1 TEASPOON SALT
½ TEASPOON PEPPER

1½ TEASPOONS DRY MUSTARD
2 CUPS SHREDDED ZUCCHINI,
 PATTED DRY
1⅓ CUPS FRESHLY GRATED PARMESAN
 CHEESE
1 TEASPOON FINELY CHOPPED
 FRESH THYME
2 EGGS, BEATEN
ABOUT ¾ CUP LOW-FAT MILK

1. Preheat the oven to 375°F. Grease a baking sheet. Put the all-purpose flour and whole wheat flour into a bowl, stir in the baking powder, salt, pepper, and dry mustard, then lightly rub in the butter until the mixture resembles bread crumbs. Stir in the zucchini, cheese, and thyme. Stir in the eggs and milk and mix to a soft dough.

2. Turn out the dough onto a lightly floured surface and lightly knead, then shape into an 8-inch circle. Put the dough onto the prepared baking sheet, then cut three fairly deep slashes in the top of the loaf with a sharp knife.

3. Bake the loaf in the preheated oven for 40-50 minutes, or until well risen and deep golden brown. Transfer to a wire rack to cool. Serve warm or cold in slices.

. . .

## Variation

*Replace the Parmesan cheese with ¾ cup freshly cooked chopped cremini mushrooms and substitute 2 tablespoons chopped fresh basil for the thyme.*

# Making Your Baking Healthier

Using vegetables in baked goods instantly raises the bar from a health point of view and makes cakes a less guilty indulgence. But what about the other ingredients? It goes without saying that you'll need sugar and fat, but there are healthier options even when it comes to these normally naughty ingredients.

DAIRY PRODUCTS AND EGGS—These are core ingredients that improve flavor and texture.

Use butter instead of margarine. Unsalted butter has a cleaner flavor and puts you in charge of the salt content. Organic cream and milk taste better and are relatively free from pesticide residues.

Organic or free-range eggs, or eggs from rare-breed hens, have a fabulous fresh flavor, superb golden yolks, and dense whites.

FLOUR—Choose the best high-quality organic wheat flour.

Whole wheat flour has more nutrients and fiber than white flour but is too heavy for cakes. However, a half-and-half mixture with white all-purpose flour works well.

Spelt and Kamut are ancient wheat varieties that are particularly good for making bread. They are used in the same way as white flour.

SUGAR—Pure, unrefined, unbleached cane sugar is perfect for baking because it adds moisture and creams easily with fats.

Superfine sugar has a fine texture that is good for most cakes, cookies, and meringues. Granulated sugar can be used instead of superfine sugar, or process it in a food processor for 1 minute to make superfine sugar.

Demerara is a raw sugar that makes a crunchy topping for crisps, cakes, and cookies.

Palm sugar adds a deep toffee flavor.

COCONUT—Once shunned as a dietary devil, coconut is now classified as a so-called "superfood" that burns body fat and keeps hunger pangs at bay. A must-have ingredient for healthier baked goods, it is available in several forms.

You can scoop the top layer of coconut cream from a can of coconut milk, and cans of coconut cream (don't confuse it with the sweetened version used for making cocktails) are now sold in some supermarkets and in Asian grocery stores. You can use coconut milk as a dairy-free replacement for cow's milk.

Coconut oil is a solid white vegetable shortening that works well as a replacement for butter in creamed cake batters.

CAKE COLORING—Vegetable juices, such as carrot, beet, or spinach, make excellent natural food colorings. You can mix the juice with marzipan to make attractive vegetable decorations, or use it to tint glazes, icings, or buttercreams.

*Beet Buttercream*
Beat 6 tablespoons unsalted butter until fluffy. Gradually beat in 1⅓ cups of sifted confectioners' sugar. Thin the mixture with 1 tablespoon of milk, then stir in 2-4 teaspoons of beet juice.

DECORATION—Vegetable leaves and seeds give a hint of what's in the cake. Feathery fennel tops and seeds are attractive and add flavor. Delicate pea shoots are also good.

## Getting the Best from Vegetables
Prep vegetables just before you use them. Cook briefly in just a little water, or, better still, steam them. You'll retain more nutrients if the vegetables aren't in direct contact with the water.

## Seasonal Eating
Vegetables are at their freshest, tastiest, and most nutritious when they are in season, especially when freshly picked. So if a recipe specifies out-of-season produce, be patient and put it on the back burner until they are in season.

# CHAPTER 2:

## Cookies, Bars & Slices

# Chocolate-Dipped Parsnip & Pistachio Cookies

Often overlooked, the versatile parsnip is a boon to bakers. Here, it is pureed and combined with pistachios, nutmeg, and lemon zest to create a unique but subtle flavor that will hit the spot if you prefer cookies that are not too sweet. They are delicious with coffee.

## Cook's Tip

Make sure you discard all the woody ends of the parsnips before steaming. Steaming is preferable to boiling when cooking root vegetables for a puree. It prevents the porous vegetables from being waterlogged during cooking.

## MAKES 18-20

### Ingredients

2 SMALL PARSNIPS, CUT INTO
  CHUNKS
1⅓ CUPS ALL-PURPOSE FLOUR,
  PLUS 1 TABLESPOON FOR DUSTING
PINCH OF SALT
⅓ CUP CONFECTIONERS' SUGAR
½ TEASPOON FRESHLY GRATED
  LEMON ZEST
¼ TEASPOON FRESHLY GRATED
  NUTMEG

1 STICK UNSALTED BUTTER,
AT ROOM TEMPERATURE, CUT
INTO CUBES
3 TABLESPOONS FINELY CHOPPED
SHELLED PISTACHIO NUTS

### Chocolate Dip

6 OUNCES SEMISWEET CHOCOLATE,
BROKEN INTO SMALL PIECES

---

1. Put the parsnips into a steamer and steam for about
10-15 minutes, until tender. Transfer to a blender or food
processor and puree until smooth.

2. Combine the flour, salt, confectioners' sugar, lemon zest,
nutmeg, and butter in the bowl of a food processor. Pulse
in 5-second bursts until a coarse dough forms. Add the
parsnip puree and pulse briefly to mix. Add the nuts and
pulse again, being careful not to overwork the dough. Scrape
the dough onto a large piece of plastic wrap. Roll into an
8-inch log. Chill in the refrigerator for 2-8 hours.

3. Preheat the oven to 375°F. Line a baking sheet with a
silicone sheet.

4. Dust the edge of a sharp knife with flour and slice the
log into ½-inch circles. Place on the prepared sheet and
bake in the preheated oven for 18-20 minutes, turning the
sheet halfway through the cooking time, until the cookies
are golden at the edges and firm to touch. Let cool on the
sheet until firm, then transfer to a wire rack.

5. To make the chocolate dip, put the chocolate into a
heatproof bowl set over a saucepan of gently simmering water
and heat until melted.

6. Lay a silicone sheet on the work surface. Dip one half of
each cookie in the chocolate. Let drip over the bowl, then
transfer to the silicone sheet to set.

...

# Corn, Coconut & Lime Cookies

*Lime juice and zest add punch to the warm, earthy flavors of these corn and coconut cookies. Because the corn is naturally sweet, you won't need to use as much sugar as in standard cookie recipes.*

MAKES 18-20

## Ingredients

2 CUPS ALL-PURPOSE FLOUR
1 CUP INSTANT GRITS
2 TEASPOONS BAKING POWDER
½ TEASPOON BAKING SODA
½ TEASPOON SALT
½ CUP COLD COCONUT OIL
1 STICK UNSALTED BUTTER
¾ CUP GRANULATED SUGAR
1 EGG, LIGHTLY BEATEN

1 CUP FROZEN CORN KERNELS, THAWED AND DRAINED
2 TABLESPOONS FINELY GRATED LIME ZEST

## Lime Icing

1⅓ CUPS CONFECTIONERS' SUGAR, SIFTED
1 TABLESPOON FINELY GRATED LIME ZEST
3 TABLESPOONS FRESHLY SQUEEZED LIME JUICE

1. Preheat the oven to 350°F. Line a large baking sheet with a silicone sheet.

2. Sift together the flour, grits, baking powder, baking soda, and salt into a large bowl.

3. Put the oil, butter, and sugar into a separate large bowl and beat with a handheld electric mixer for 3-5 minutes, until light and fluffy. Gradually beat in the flour mixture and the egg.

4. Puree the corn in a blender until smooth, then add to the mixture with the lime zest.

5. Spoon heaping tablespoons of the dough on the prepared sheet, spaced 4 inches apart. Flatten the mounds slightly with the back of a spoon.

6. Bake the cookies in the preheated oven for 15-18 minutes, turning the sheet halfway through the cooking time, until the edges are just beginning to brown.

7. Carefully transfer to a wire rack and let cool completely.

8. To make the icing, combine all the ingredients in a bowl and spoon a little over the top of each cookie.

. . .

## Cook's Tip

*These delicious cookies will keep in an airtight container for up to a week, but they are most delicious when eaten on the day of baking.*

# Pumpkin Whoopie Pies

*Just when you thought whoopie pies couldn't get any more indulgent—the rich, silky-textured pumpkin puree is perfectly complemented by the rich cinnamon and maple syrup filling.*

MAKES 12

## Ingredients

2¼ CUPS ALL-PURPOSE FLOUR
½ TEASPOON BAKING POWDER
½ TEASPOON BAKING SODA
1½ TEASPOONS GROUND CINNAMON
¼ TEASPOON SALT
1 CUP FIRMLY PACKED LIGHT
  BROWN SUGAR
½ CUP SUNFLOWER OIL
1 EXTRA-LARGE EGG, BEATEN
1 TEASPOON VANILLA EXTRACT
½ CUP CANNED PUMPKIN PUREE

### Cinnamon & Maple Syrup Filling

1 CUP CREAM CHEESE
6 TABLESPOONS UNSALTED BUTTER,
  SOFTENED
2 TABLESPOONS MAPLE SYRUP
1 TEASPOON GROUND CINNAMON
⅔ CUP CONFECTIONERS' SUGAR,
  SIFTED

*1.* Preheat the oven to 350°F. Line two or three large baking sheets with wax paper. Sift together the flour, baking powder, baking soda, cinnamon, and salt.

*2.* Put the sugar and oil into a large bowl and beat with a handheld electric mixer for 1 minute. Whisk in the egg and vanilla extract, then beat in the pumpkin puree. Stir in the sifted flour mixture and beat until thoroughly incorporated.

*3.* Pipe or spoon 24 mounds of the batter onto the prepared baking sheets, spaced well apart to allow for spreading. Bake, one sheet at a time, in the preheated oven for 8-10 minutes, until risen and just firm to the touch. Let cool for 5 minutes, then, using a spatula, transfer to a wire rack and let cool completely.

*4.* For the filling, put the cream cheese and butter into a bowl and beat until well blended. Beat in the maple syrup, cinnamon, and confectioners' sugar until smooth.

*5.* To assemble, spread or pipe the filling over the flat side of half the cakes. Top with the remaining cakes.

...

## Cook's Tip

*You can make the filling in advance, but don't assemble the cakes until just before you're ready to serve so that they don't become soggy.*

# Sweet Potato Brownies

*Sweet potatoes make amazingly gooey, sweet brownies. Once you have tried these, there's no doubt that you will want to bake them again and again.*

MAKES 12

## Ingredients

1 TABLESPOON OLIVE OIL,
  FOR OILING
1 SWEET POTATO, SHREDDED
⅔ CUP OLIVE OIL
½ CUP STEVIA
⅔ CUP UNSWEETENED COCOA POWDER
½ TEASPOON BAKING POWDER
½ TEASPOON BAKING SODA
½ CUP GROUND ALMONDS
  (ALMOND MEAL)
2 EGGS, BEATEN

3 TABLESPOONS COARSELY CHOPPED
  WALNUTS

1. Preheat the oven to 350°F. Lightly oil a shallow 7½-inch square cake pan, then line it with a large square of parchment paper, snipping into the corners diagonally and pressing the paper into the pan to line the bottom and sides.

2. Put the sweet potato, oil, stevia, cocoa powder, baking powder, baking soda, almonds, eggs, and walnuts into a large bowl and stir well. Pour the batter into the prepared pan. Bake for 20 minutes, or until well risen and the center is just set.

3. Let cool in the pan for 15 minutes. Lift out of the pan, using the parchment paper, then carefully remove the paper. Cut into 12 brownies to serve.

...

## Cook's Tip

*If this recipe is too chocolaty for your taste, reduce the amount of cocoa to ⅓ cup.*

# Squash, Lemon & Fennel Cookies

## MAKES 8

### Ingredients

2 CUPS PEELED, SEEDED, AND
  DICED BUTTERNUT, ACORN, OR
  OTHER WINTER SQUASH
1 TABLESPOON FENNEL SEEDS
1¾ CUPS ALL-PURPOSE FLOUR,
  PLUS 1 TABLESPOON FOR DUSTING
¼ CUP SUPERFINE SUGAR
1½ TEASPOONS BAKING POWDER
½ TEASPOON SALT
¼ TEASPOON BAKING SODA
1 STICK UNSALTED BUTTER,
  AT ROOM TEMPERATURE,
  CUT INTO CUBES
⅓ CUP BUTTERMILK
FINELY GRATED ZEST OF 1 LEMON

### Lemon & Fennel Icing

1 CUP CONFECTIONERS' SUGAR,
  SIFTED
1 TABLESPOON WATER
1½ TEASPOONS LEMON JUICE

1. Preheat the oven to 375°F. Line a baking sheet with a silicone sheet.

2. Put the squash into the top part of a steamer and steam for 10-15 minutes, until tender. Blend to a puree in the small bowl of a food processor, frequently scraping down the sides. Push the puree through a strainer into a bowl and set aside until needed.

3. Put the fennel seeds into a dry skillet and cook over medium-high heat for 30 seconds until they smell toasty. Immediately transfer them to a plate, then lightly crush in a mortar with a pestle.

4. Combine the flour, sugar, baking powder, salt, baking soda, and butter in the bowl of a food processor. Pulse briefly until the mixture resembles coarse crumbs.

5. Add the squash puree, buttermilk, lemon zest, and 2 teaspoons of the fennel seeds and pulse in short bursts until mixed.

6. Turn out the mixture onto a floured board and use a well-floured rolling pin to roll out to a thickness of ¾ inch. Cut into eight circles, using a 2½-inch cutter. Arrange the circles on the prepared sheet, ¾ inch apart.

7. Bake in the preheated oven for 20-25 minutes, turning the sheet halfway through the cooking time, until pale golden and risen. Transfer to a wire rack and let cool.

8. To make the icing, mix the confectioners' sugar, water, and lemon juice together. Stir in the remaining toasted fennel seeds. Spoon the icing over the cookies and let set. Eat the cookies on the day of making.

...

# Celeriac, Lemon & Cardamom Oat Bars

## MAKES 12

### Ingredients

1¼ STICKS UNSALTED BUTTER,
  PLUS 1 TABLESPOON FOR GREASING
2 CUPS ROLLED OATS
1 CUP INSTANT OATS
1 CUP SHREDDED CELERIAC
FINELY GRATED ZEST OF 1 LEMON
SEEDS FROM 7 CARDAMOM PODS,
  CRUSHED
¼ CUP DEMERARA OR OTHER
  RAW SUGAR
3 TABLESPOONS LIGHT CORN SYRUP
PINCH OF SALT

1. Preheat the oven to 375°F. Grease a 9½ x 7-inch baking pan and line with parchment paper, pushing it into the corners to line the bottom and sides.

2. Put the rolled oats, instant oats, celeriac, lemon zest, and cardamom seeds into a large bowl and mix to combine.

3. Put the butter, sugar, corn syrup, and salt into a saucepan and heat, stirring, over medium heat until the butter is melted.

4. Add the oat mixture to the pan, stirring well to combine.

5. Transfer the dough to the prepared pan and firmly press flat, making sure the corners and edges are firm.

6. Bake in the preheated oven for 25 minutes, until golden and firm. Remove from the oven and let cool in the pan for 10 minutes. Slice into 12 rectangles while still in the pan. Let stand until completely cool and set, then turn out of the pan and break into rectangles.

...

## Cook's Tip

It is important to let the oat bars stand in the pan until completely cold. If you try to lift them out sooner, they will crumble and turn into granola. Press the dough firmly into the pan before baking.

# Honeyed Carrot & Pecan Squares

*This cake is packed with vitamin A-boosting carrots, vitamin B- and mineral-boosting wheat germ, and energy-boosting whole wheat flour.*

## MAKES 15

### Ingredients

3 EGGS
⅔ CUP VIRGIN OLIVE OIL
½ CUP FIRMLY PACKED LIGHT
  BROWN SUGAR
⅓ CUP SET HONEY
1½ CUPS WHOLE WHEAT FLOUR
¼ CUP WHEAT GERM
2 TEASPOONS BAKING POWDER
2 TEASPOONS GROUND GINGER
GRATED ZEST OF 1 ORANGE
1¼ TEASPOONS GROUND ALLSPICE
8 CARROTS, SHREDDED

½ CUP BROKEN PECAN PIECES
GRATED ORANGE ZEST AND PECAN
  PIECES, TO DECORATE (OPTIONAL)

### Frosting

½ CUP GREEK-STYLE YOGURT
⅔ CUP CREAM CHEESE

1. Preheat the oven to 350°F. Line a nonstick 7 x 11-inch baking pan with parchment paper, snipping into the corners diagonally and pressing it into the pan, so that the bottom and sides are lined.

2. Crack the eggs into a large bowl, add the oil, sugar, and ¼ cup of the honey, and whisk until smooth. Put the flour, wheat germ, and baking powder into a small bowl, then add the ginger, orange zest, and 1 teaspoon of the allspice and stir. Add the dry ingredients to the egg mixture and beat until smooth. Add the carrots and nuts and stir.

3. Spoon the batter into the prepared pan and spread it in an even layer. Bake in the preheated oven for 30-35 minutes, or until well risen and a toothpick when inserted into the center comes out clean.

4. Turn the cake out of the pan, peel off the parchment paper, and transfer to a wire rack to cool completely.

5. To make the frosting, put the yogurt, cream cheese, and the remaining honey and allspice into a bowl and beat together until smooth. Spread the frosting over the cake, then sprinkle with orange zest and pecan pieces, if using. Cut it into 15 squares and serve.

...

## Cook's Tip

*You can use 3 shredded raw beets in place of the carrots.*

# Rhubarb & Lemon Drizzle Squares

*Sometimes only a piece of cake will make you happy—this brown rice flour and ground almond cake is perfect for an almost guilt-free midafternoon pick-me-up.*

MAKES 9

## Ingredients

6 YOUNG RHUBARB STALKS, TRIMMED
  AND CUT INTO ¾-INCH SLICES
1 CUP GROUND ALMONDS
  (ALMOND MEAL)
¾ CUP BROWN RICE FLOUR
1½ TEASPOONS BAKING POWDER
1 RIPE BANANA, MASHED
⅔ CUP RICE BRAN OIL
½ CUP FIRMLY PACKED LIGHT
  BROWN SUGAR

GRATED ZEST OF 1 LEMON
3 EGGS
¼ CUP UNBLANCHED ALMONDS,
  COARSELY CHOPPED

## Syrup

JUICE OF 2 LEMONS
⅓ CUP FIRMLY PACKED LIGHT
  BROWN SUGAR

1. Preheat the oven to 350°F. Line a 12 x 8 x 1½-inch square cake pan with a large piece of nonstick parchment paper, snipping it into the corners diagonally to line the bottom and sides of the pan.

2. Put the rhubarb into a dry roasting pan and bake in the preheated oven for 10 minutes, until almost soft. Remove from the oven but do not turn the oven off.

3. Put the ground almonds, flour, and baking powder into a bowl and stir together.

4. Put the banana, oil, sugar, and lemon zest into a separate bowl and whisk together until smooth. Whisk in the eggs, one at a time, then beat in the flour mixture.

5. Spoon the batter into the prepared pan, then sprinkle the rhubarb over the top. Bake for 25-30 minutes, until the cake is well risen and springs back when pressed with a fingertip.

6. To make the syrup, mix the lemon juice with the sugar. Spoon half the syrup over the hot cake and let soak for 1-2 minutes. Spoon the remaining syrup over the cake, then sprinkle with the chopped almonds and let cool in the pan.

7. Lift the cake out of the pan, peel away the paper, and cut into 9 squares. Eat within 2 days or freeze until needed.

. . .

## Cook's Tip

*Freeze the whole cake in the pan for 1-2 hours. Transfer to a plastic bag to finish freezing. Cut into squares before it's completely thawed.*

# Cauliflower & Apricot Swirl Cheesecake Bars

Combined with low-fat cream cheese, creamy yogurt, and tangy dried apricots, cauliflower is the mystery ingredient in these unusual cheesecake bars. The crunchy oat crust and colorful swirled apricot topping are perfect with the creamy filling.

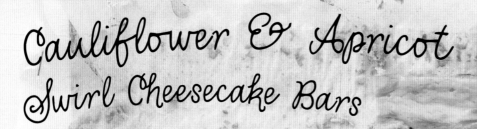

## Cook's Tip

The apricot puree should be of a pouring consistency. You can add a little water if it seems to be too thick.

MAKES 16

## Ingredients

1 TABLESPOON OIL, FOR OILING
2 CUPS DRIED APRICOTS
JUICE OF 1 LARGE ORANGE
2 CUPS LOW-FAT COTTAGE CHEESE
1¾ CUPS PLAIN YOGURT
1 CUP SUPERFINE SUGAR
1 TABLESPOON VANILLA EXTRACT
4 EGGS, LIGHTLY BEATEN
½ CUP ALL-PURPOSE FLOUR
1 CUP SMALL CAULIFLOWER FLORETS
  (WITHOUT STEMS), FINELY CHOPPED

## Crust

2⅓ CUPS WHOLE WHEAT FLOUR
⅔ CUP ROLLED OATS
FINELY GRATED ZEST OF
  1 LARGE ORANGE
¼ CUP HONEY
1¼ STICKS UNSALTED BUTTER

1. Lightly oil a 12 x 9½-inch roasting pan and line with parchment paper. Preheat the oven to 350°F.

2. To make the crust, mix the flour and oats together. Put the orange zest, honey, and butter into a saucepan over medium heat and heat until melted. Stir into the dry ingredients.

3. Transfer the dough to the prepared pan and firmly press flat. Make sure the corners and edges are firm. Bake in the preheated oven for 15 minutes, until crisp.

4. Meanwhile, put the apricots into a small saucepan with the orange juice and enough water to cover by about ¾ inch. Bring to a boil, then simmer gently over medium heat for 7 minutes, or until soft. Put into a blender or food processor. Puree until smooth, then push through a strainer into a bowl and set aside until needed.

5. Remove the crust from the oven and set aside. Reduce the oven temperature to 325°F.

6. Put the cheese, yogurt, sugar, and vanilla extract into a bowl and beat with a handheld electric mixer until creamy. Beat in the eggs and flour, then gently stir in the chopped cauliflower.

7. Mix half the apricot puree with the cauliflower mixture and pour over the crust. Swirl the remaining puree attractively over the top, being careful to avoid overmixing it.

8. Bake for 1-1¼ hours, or until a toothpick inserted in the center comes out clean. Let cool completely in the pan, then chill in the refrigerator for 2-8 hours before removing from the pan. Slice into 16 bars.

...

# Potato & Black Pepper Oat Cakes

Comforting mashed potatoes and a good grinding of black pepper add the wow factor to these delectable oat cakes. Pleasantly chewy but crisp at the edges, they are equally delicious plain or served with butter.

MAKES 9

## Ingredients

2 TABLESPOONS BUTTER, PLUS
 ½ TABLESPOON FOR GREASING
2 RUSSET POTATOES, CUT INTO
 CHUNKS
¼ TEASPOON SALT
½ TEASPOON PEPPER
⅓ CUP STEEL-CUT OATS
⅓ CUP ROLLED OATS
1 TABLESPOON ALL-PURPOSE FLOUR,
 FOR DUSTING

1. Preheat the oven to 400°F. Line a baking sheet with a silicone sheet or well-greased parchment paper.

2. Bring a large saucepan of water to a boil. Add the potatoes, bring back to a boil, and cook for 10 minutes, until tender.

3. Drain the potatoes, then return them to the pan and cover with a clean dish towel. Let stand for 5 minutes to absorb the excess moisture. Mash until smooth, then stir in the butter, salt, pepper, steel-cut oats, and rolled oats.

4. Pack the dough together well and turn out onto a well-floured board. Using a well-floured rolling pin, roll out the dough to a thickness of ¼ inch.

5. Cut into circles with a 2¾-inch cutter. Lift the circles carefully onto the prepared sheet, using a spatula. Reroll and cut the scraps until all the dough is used.

6. Bake in the preheated oven for 20 minutes, turning the sheet halfway through the cooking time, until the cakes are golden at the edges. Remove from the oven. Let cool on the sheet until firm, then carefully transfer to a wire rack to cool completely.

...

## Cook's Tip

For the best flavor, it is well worth using fresh, good-quality peppercorns. Don't be tempted to use already-ground pepper—it doesn't have the appetizing aroma of freshly ground pepper.

# Roasted Cauliflower Frittata Slices

Made with green cauliflower (use white cauliflower if you can't find green), tomatoes, and scallions, this colorful vegetable frittata hits the spot at any time of day. Serve with a salad for a light lunch, dinner, or Sunday brunch. Leftovers are great for a picnic.

SERVES 8

*Ingredients*

1 HEAD GREEN CAULIFLOWER,
  OUTER LEAVES REMOVED
½ CUP OLIVE OIL
1 TEASPOON SALT
¾ TEASPOON PEPPER
1 ONION, CHOPPED
1 TEASPOON FRESH THYME LEAVES
8 EGGS
⅓ CUP CHOPPED FRESH FLAT-LEAF
  PARSLEY
1 CUP ALL-PURPOSE FLOUR
1½ TEASPOONS BAKING POWDER
1 CUP SHREDDED SHARP CHEDDAR
  CHEESE
1 LARGE SCALLION, SOME GREEN
  INCLUDED, THINLY SLICED
  DIAGONALLY
3 SMALL RIPE TOMATOES, SLICED
¼ CUP COARSELY GRATED PARMESAN
  CHEESE

*1.* Preheat the oven to 425°F. Line a 10½ x 8½-inch baking pan with parchment paper.

*2.* Slice the cauliflower lengthwise into quarters, discarding the tough centered stem. Slice into small florets. Spread out in a roasting pan. Sprinkle with 3 tablespoons of the oil, ¾ teaspoon of the salt, and ½ teaspoon of the pepper.

*3.* Cover tightly with aluminum foil and roast in the preheated oven for 15 minutes. Remove the foil, stir, and roast for an additional 10 minutes, or until golden at the edges. Remove from the oven and let cool. Reduce the oven temperature to 350°F.

*4.* Meanwhile, heat 2 tablespoons of the remaining oil in a skillet. Add the onion and thyme and sauté over medium heat for about 10 minutes, until soft, then remove from the heat and let cool.

*5.* In a large bowl, beat the eggs with the remaining oil, the onion mixture, and the parsley. Whisk in the flour, baking powder, and the remaining salt and pepper. Stir in the cheddar cheese and cauliflower.

*6.* Pour the mixture into the prepared baking pan. Sprinkle the scallion and tomatoes over the top, then sprinkle with the Parmesan cheese. Bake for 30 minutes, or until a knife inserted into the center comes out clean.

*7.* Remove from the oven and let cool in the pan for 15 minutes. Turn out and serve warm or at room temperature.

...

# Your Very Own Vegetables

One of the best things about growing your own vegetables is being able to enjoy the fruits of your labor afterward. It's hard to beat the sense of achievement you get from picking crops from your own garden and enjoying their unique flavor and freshness in your baked goods. Growing your own produce is becoming increasingly popular, because more people want to know exactly where their food has come from, and to make sure it is as natural and pesticide-free as possible. Growing your own is also the best way of being sure that you get maximum nutrients from your fruit and vegetables.

## Here are a few things to consider when growing your own...

### What to Grow?

A good place to start is to grow something you actually enjoy eating. There's no point having a row of succulent beets if no one in your family likes them. Consider growing produce that is expensive to buy or difficult to find, such as young fava beans, the more unusual winter squash, or heirloom tomatoes.

### How Much to Grow?

You can easily start off with a few containers or a small area of your yard. However, if you want to become truly self-sufficient, you must be prepared to invest plenty of space, time, and care. It is also a good idea to plan what you grow carefully, to avoid ending up with a bumper crop of fruit and vegetables that you won't be able to use.

### Preparing an Area

You'll need to prepare the area that you are going to use. Remove all weeds and prepare the soil. Leaf mold and well-rotted organic matter can be dug into the soil or spread across the surface. Their bulk will improve the drainage of heavy soil and allow dry soil to hold onto moisture and valuable nutrients.

### Growing Organically

Pests are always a problem—you will probably find that there is an endless variety of animals intent on devouring your efforts. Many gardeners now prefer to use organic gardening techniques instead of chemicals or fertilizers. To avoid using herbicides, you can control weeds by spreading bark mulch, leaf mold, or a black plastic sheet across the soil. Use biological pest control instead of chemical sprays.

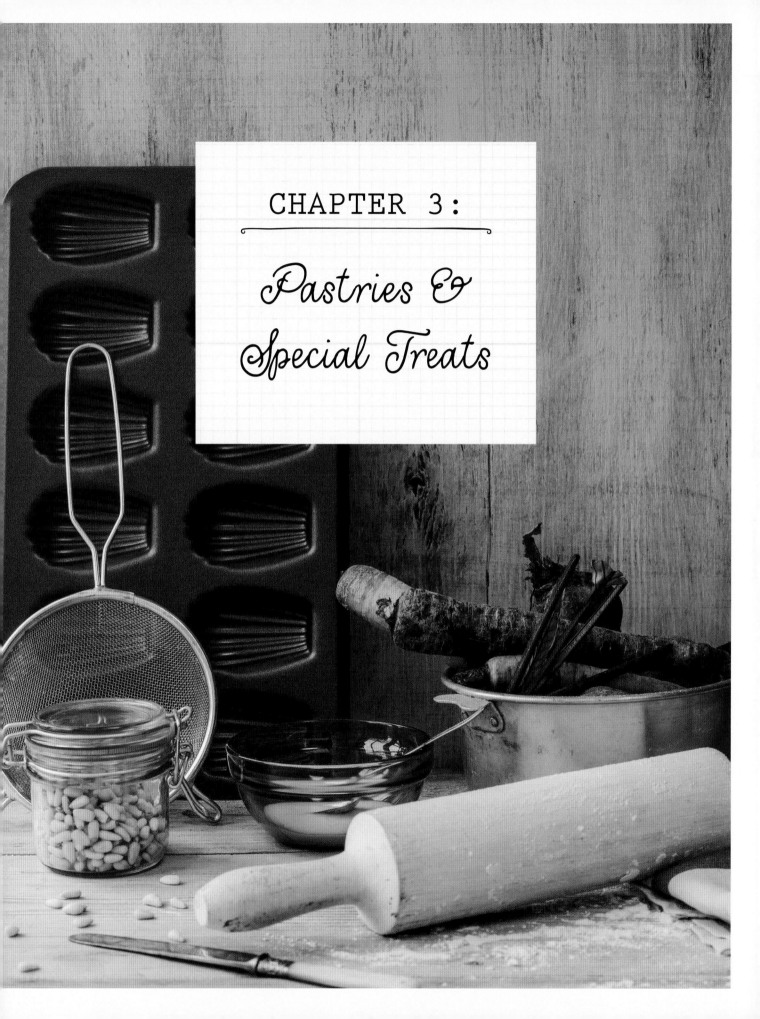

# CHAPTER 3:

## Pastries &
## Special Treats

# Swiss Chard Tart with Orange, Pine Nuts & Raisins

Packed with vitamins and minerals, Swiss chard has enormous leaves with a rich, complex flavor. Cooked down to a soft puree and mixed with ricotta cheese, crunchy pine nuts, and dried fruit, they make a deliciously moist tart that is surprisingly sweet, although it contains little sugar.

## Cook's Tip

Place the ricotta cheese on a large square of damp cheesecloth. Gather up the corners and tie with string. Tie to the handle of a wooden spoon and suspend over a deep bowl. Let drain in a cool place for at least 2 hours or overnight.

**SERVES 6-8**

## Ingredients

¼ CUP RAISINS

1 TABLESPOON OIL, FOR OILING

3¼ POUNDS SWISS CHARD, STEMS
AND CENTERED RIB DISCARDED

1 SHEET PREPARED ROLLED
DOUGH PIE CRUST

1 TABLESPOON FLOUR, FOR DUSTING

2 EXTRA-LARGE EGGS

3 TABLESPOONS GRANULATED SUGAR

¼ TEASPOON GRATED NUTMEG

2 PINCHES OF SALT

1 CUP RICOTTA CHEESE, DRAINED

1 (1¼-OUNCE) PIECE CANDIED
ORANGE PEEL, HALF FINELY
CHOPPED, HALF SLICED INTO
THIN SLIVERS

⅓ CUP PINE NUTS, TOASTED

1 TABLESPOON CONFECTIONERS' SUGAR,
FOR DUSTING

---

*1.* Cover the raisins with boiling water and let soak for 30 minutes, then drain. Preheat the oven to 325°F. Oil a 9½-inch loose-bottom tart pan.

*2.* Put the chard leaves into a large saucepan without any extra water. Cover and simmer over medium heat for about 10 minutes, stirring frequently, until thoroughly wilted. Drain, squeezing with your hands to remove as much liquid as possible. Finely chop and set aside.

*3.* Thinly roll out the dough on a well-floured surface and use to line the prepared pan. Press a rolling pin over the rim to remove surplus dough (reserve the scraps). Use the side of your index finger to press the dough into the edge of the bottom of the pan to raise it slightly above the rim. Line the bottom with aluminum foil and fill with pie weights or dried beans.

*4.* Bake in the preheated oven for 10 minutes. Remove the foil and weights, then bake for an additional 5 minutes. Remove from the oven. Increase the oven temperature to 350°F. Put a baking sheet into the oven to heat.

*5.* In a large bowl, whisk together the eggs, sugar, nutmeg, and salt. Stir in the ricotta cheese, chopped orange peel, pine nuts, raisins, and chard. Spoon the filling into the pastry shell. Roll out the scraps and cut into small stars, crescents, or diamonds. Place on top of the filling and cover loosely with aluminum foil. Bake for 20 minutes. Remove the foil and bake for an additional 10-15 minutes.

*6.* Let the tart cool in the pan for 15 minutes, then remove from the pan and transfer to a serving plate. Dust with the confectioners' sugar and decorate with the orange peel slivers. Serve warm or at room temperature.

...

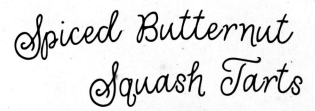

# Spiced Butternut Squash Tarts

*These individual tarts have all the flavor of pumpkin pie. You can use other winter squash in place of the butternut squash. For an indulgent dessert, serve with whipped cream or vanilla ice cream.*

## MAKES 4

### Ingredients

½ TABLESPOON BUTTER, PLUS
  ½ TABLESPOON FOR GREASING
3 CUPS PEELED AND SEEDED
  ½-INCH BUTTERNUT SQUASH PIECES
1 TABLESPOON MAPLE SYRUP
½ PIECE OF PRESERVED GINGER
  IN SYRUP, FINELY CHOPPED
¼ TEASPOON CINNAMON
¼ TEASPOON ALLSPICE
6 SHEETS PHYLLO PASTRY
2 TABLESPOONS OIL, FOR BRUSHING
1 TABLESPOON CONFECTIONERS' SUGAR,
  FOR DUSTING

### Cook's Tip

*Always dust confectioners' sugar over open tarts at the last minute before serving—otherwise the sugar will be absorbed by the filling and the tarts will look less attractive.*

---

1. Preheat the oven to 375°F. Lightly grease four 4-inch tart pans.

2. Put the squash onto a baking sheet and dot with the butter. Roast in the preheated oven for 5 minutes, then stir and return to the oven for an additional 20 minutes, or until the squash is beginning to brown.

3. Stir the maple syrup, ginger, cinnamon, and allspice into the squash and cook for an additional 5 minutes. Let cool.

4. Cut the pastry into twelve 4-inch squares. Brush four of the squares with oil. Place a second sheet of pastry on top of each, at an angle to the first so that the points of the squares do not align; you are aiming to create a star shape. Brush with oil again and repeat with the remaining pastry sheets to make four stacks, each with three layers.

5. Transfer the pastry stacks into the prepared pans, press down gently, and bake in the preheated oven for 8–10 minutes, or until crisp and golden.

6. Fill the pastry shells with the squash mixture. Dust the tarts with the confectioners' sugar and serve immediately.

...

# Carrot, Fruit & Cardamom Rolls

The ever-versatile carrot takes center stage in these delicious Scandinavian-style rolls. Bursting with candied fruit and lightly spiced with cardamom, they can't be beat by store-bought rolls. Enjoy them freshly baked; otherwise wrap in a clean dish towel and store in an airtight container for up to two days.

## Variation

You can use sugar pearls instead of confectioners' sugar for a more dramatic finish. Dust it over the rolls while they are still warm.

MAKES 16

*Ingredients*

2 LARGE CARROTS
2¾ CUPS WHITE BREAD FLOUR,
  SIFTED, PLUS 1 TABLESPOON
  FOR DUSTING
2 TABLESPOONS ACTIVE DRY YEAST
3 TABLESPOONS SUPERFINE SUGAR
2 TEASPOONS GROUND CARDAMOM
  SEEDS (FROM ABOUT 24 PODS)

½ TEASPOON SALT
1 STICK UNSALTED BUTTER
1 EGG, LIGHTLY BEATEN
⅓ CUP LUKEWARM MILK
1 TABLESPOON OIL, FOR OILING
1 CUP CHOPPED CANDIED FRUIT
1 EGG YOLK
1 TABLESPOON COLD MILK
1 TABLESPOON CONFECTIONERS'
  SUGAR, FOR SPRINKLING

1. Put the carrots into the top of a steamer and steam for
15 minutes, until tender, then puree in a blender until
smooth. Set aside until needed.

2. Line a baking sheet with a silicone sheet. Put the flour,
yeast, superfine sugar, cardamom, and salt into a large bowl
and mix to combine. Melt all but 2 tablespoons of the butter
and let cool slightly. Mix the beaten egg with the lukewarm
milk and the melted butter. Stir into the flour mixture,
then add the carrot puree. Mix to a soft dough.

3. Turn out the dough onto a floured board and knead for
10-15 minutes, until silky. Transfer to a lightly oiled
bowl, cover with plastic wrap, and let stand in a warm place
for 1½-2 hours, or until doubled in size. Turn out onto a
floured board and punch down to get rid of the air. Roll out
thinly to a 17½ x 12-inch rectangle.

4. Melt the remaining butter and brush it over the surface of
the dough. Sprinkle with the candied fruit, taking it right
to the edge of the dough and breaking up any clumps.

5. Roll up the dough from the long edge into a log. Slice into
1-inch circles and place on the prepared baking sheet. Cover
with plastic wrap and let stand for 30 minutes. Meanwhile,
preheat the oven to 400°F.

6. Mix the egg yolk with the cold milk and brush over the
rolls, then bake in the preheated oven for 10-15 minutes,
until golden.

7. Transfer to a wire rack to cool, then sprinkle with the
confectioners' sugar. The rolls are best eaten freshly baked.

...

# Beet Madeleines with Spiced Icing

**MAKES 22-24**

## Ingredients

3 GOLDEN BEETS, PEELED AND CUT
  INTO ¾-INCH CUBES
¾ CUP ALL-PURPOSE FLOUR, PLUS
  1 TABLESPOON FOR DUSTING
1 TEASPOON BAKING POWDER
PINCH OF SALT
2 EXTRA-LARGE EGGS
⅓ CUP SUPERFINE SUGAR
2 TABLESPOONS HONEY
5 TABLESPOONS UNSALTED BUTTER,
  MELTED AND COOLED SLIGHTLY
1 TEASPOON FINELY GRATED
  ORANGE ZEST
1 TABLESPOON OIL, FOR OILING

## Icing

1¼ CUPS CONFECTIONERS' SUGAR
2½ TABLESPOONS FRESHLY SQUEEZED
  ORANGE JUICE
2½ CUPS PEELED AND CHOPPED
  FRESH GINGER

1. Put the beets into the top of a steamer and steam for 15 minutes, or until tender. Puree in a mini food processor, frequently scraping down the sides. Push through a strainer into a bowl and set aside until needed.

2. Sift together the flour, baking powder, and salt into a bowl. Put the eggs and sugar into a large bowl and beat for 5 minutes, or until creamy. Add the honey and beat for an additional minute.

3. Fold the dry ingredients into the egg mixture. Stir in the butter, orange zest, and beet puree. Transfer to a smaller bowl, cover with plastic wrap laid directly on the surface, and chill in the refrigerator for 4-8 hours.

4. Preheat the oven to 400°F. Oil two 12-section madeleine pans. Dust well with flour, shaking out the excess. Drop a tablespoon of batter into each section.

5. Bake on the middle shelf of the preheated oven for about 10 minutes, until golden, or until a knife inserted into the center of a madeleine comes out clean. Turn out onto a wire rack and let cool slightly.

6. To make the icing, put the confectioners' sugar and orange juice into a shallow bowl and mix to combine. Put the chopped ginger into a garlic press and squeeze the juice into the confectioners' sugar mixture and stir to combine.

7. When the madeleines are cool enough to handle, immerse them in the icing, one at a time. Let drip over the bowl, then transfer to a wire rack and let stand until the icing has soaked in.

...

# Salted Chocolate Éclairs with Cardamom & Ricotta Cream Filling

**MAKES 10-12**

## Ingredients

### Filling
1 SMALL CARROT, SHREDDED
¾ CUP RICOTTA CHEESE
2 TABLESPOONS HEAVY CREAM
4 TEASPOONS GRANULATED SUGAR
SEEDS FROM 2 CARDAMOM PODS,
 CRUSHED
PINCH OF SALT

### Choux Pastry Dough
1 CUP WHITE BREAD FLOUR
¾ CUP WATER
1 STICK UNSALTED BUTTER, DICED
PINCH OF SALT
3 EXTRA-LARGE EGGS, LIGHTLY
 BEATEN
1 EGG WHITE (OPTIONAL)

### Topping
3 OUNCES SEMISWEET CHOCOLATE,
 BROKEN INTO SMALL PIECES
SEA SALT FLAKES, FOR SPRINKLING
(OPTIONAL)

1. Preheat the oven to 400°F. Line a baking sheet with a silicone sheet. Fit a pastry bag with a ¾-inch plain tip.

2. To make the filling, combine all the ingredients in a bowl. Let stand for 30 minutes to let the flavors develop.

3. Meanwhile, to make the dough, sift the flour twice onto a plate. Put the water, butter, and salt into a saucepan and bring to a boil. Remove from the heat and add the flour. Beat to a smooth paste that just pulls away from the side of the pan. Let stand until just warm to touch. Beat in the eggs, 1 spoonful at a time. If the mixture is too thick, add a little egg white.

4. Spoon the dough into the prepared pastry bag. Pipe a 4½-inch line of dough onto the prepared baking sheet. Immediately pipe back over the line to create a double thickness. Repeat with the remaining dough, leaving a 2-inch space between each line.

5. Bake in the preheated oven for 15 minutes, until puffed and golden, without opening the oven door. Reduce the heat to 350°F and bake for an additional 10 minutes, until crisp at the sides as well as on top.

6. Remove from the oven and immediately pierce the side of each éclair to let the steam escape. Let cool completely.

7. Slice the cooled éclairs down one side. Spoon the filling over the bottom of each éclair. Replace the tops of the éclairs and transfer to a wire rack.

8. To make the topping, put the chocolate into a heatproof bowl set over a saucepan of gently simmering water and heat until melted. Spoon the chocolate over the éclairs and sprinkle with a few sea salt flakes, if using.

...

# Baked Pumpkin Donuts

Pumpkin is a great ingredient in any baker's repertoire, lending itself particularly well to cakes and pies. Smooth pumpkin puree gives these light baked donuts a great color and deliciously moist texture.

## MAKES 6

### Ingredients

4 TABLESPOONS BUTTER, SOFTENED,
  PLUS 1 TABLESPOON FOR GREASING
1 CUP ALL-PURPOSE FLOUR
1½ TEASPOONS BAKING POWDER
½ TEASPOON SALT
1 TEASPOON GROUND CINNAMON
½ TEASPOON GRATED NUTMEG
¼ CUP FIRMLY PACKED LIGHT
  BROWN SUGAR

1 EXTRA-LARGE EGG, BEATEN
1 TEASPOON VANILLA EXTRACT
1 TABLESPOON MILK
½ CUP CANNED PUMPKIN PUREE

### Glaze

1 CUP CONFECTIONERS' SUGAR
½ TEASPOON GROUND CINNAMON
2 TABLESPOONS MILK
1-2 TEASPOONS MAPLE SYRUP

1. Preheat the oven to 375°F. Grease a 6-section donut pan.

2. Sift together the flour and baking powder into a bowl and stir in the salt, cinnamon, and nutmeg. Put the butter and sugar into a separate bowl and beat together until pale and creamy. Gradually beat in the egg, vanilla extract, and milk. Fold in the flour mixture and pumpkin puree.

3. Spoon the dough into a large pastry bag fitted with a plain tip and pipe into the prepared pan. Bake in the preheated oven for 15 minutes, until risen, golden, and just firm to the touch. Let cool for 5 minutes, then turn out onto a wire rack to cool completely.

4. To make the glaze, sift together the confectioners' sugar and cinnamon into a bowl, add the milk and maple syrup, and stir until smooth. Dip the top of each donut in the glaze and let set.

...

## Variation

If you would prefer a spicier hit of flavor, you could replace the nutmeg with an equal quantity of ground ginger or ½ teaspoon of grated fresh ginger.

# Sweet Potato & Pecan Phyllo Packages

These crisp phyllo packages are filled with a spicy mix of silky sweet potato and crunchy pecans. Coconut sugar is used as a sweetener—it has an intense flavor so you will need only a small amount. Completely versatile, these can be served freshly baked as a snack or with whipped cream as a dessert.

## Cook's Tip

This recipe uses standard phyllo sheets of 10½ x 8 inches. However, if you find larger sheets, just trim off the excess and discard. If you find sheets 16 inches long, use one long strip per package.

MAKES 12

## Ingredients

1 LARGE SWEET POTATO, BAKED,
  PEELED, AND MASHED
⅔ CUP FINELY CHOPPED PECANS
⅛ TEASPOON FRESHLY GROUND
  NUTMEG
1½ TEASPOONS FINELY CHOPPED
  FRESH GINGER
4 TEASPOONS COCONUT SUGAR

1 TEASPOON LEMON JUICE
8 PHYLLO PASTRY SHEETS
1 TABLESPOON HAZELNUT OR
OLIVE OIL, FOR BRUSHING
1 TABLESPOON CONFECTIONERS'
SUGAR MIXED WITH ½ TEASPOON
GROUND CINNAMON, FOR DUSTING

1. Preheat the oven to 400°F. Line a baking sheet with a
silicone sheet.

2. Mix the sweet potato and half the nuts together in a bowl.
Add the nutmeg, ginger, sugar, and lemon juice, mixing well
with a fork.

3. Unroll the sheets of phyllo pastry and stack on a board
with the long edge facing you. Using a ruler as a guide,
slice crossways into three 8 x 3½-inch strips. Work with one
strip at a time, covering the remaining strips with a clean
damp dish towel to prevent them from drying out.

4. Lightly brush the upper surface of one phyllo strip with
oil. Lightly sprinkle with a few of the remaining nuts.

5. Place a tablespoon of the sweet potato mixture in the
bottom left-hand corner of the pastry strip and lightly mold
it into a coarse triangle. Fold the pastry over diagonally
to form a triangle. Continue to fold in triangles until you
reach the end of the strip. Wrap a second strip around the
package, continuing to fold over diagonally into a triangle.

6. Brush both sides of the package with oil and place on the
baking sheet. Repeat with the remaining 22 phyllo strips.

7. Bake in the preheated oven for 10-12 minutes, turning
halfway through the cooking time, or until golden and crisp.

8. Transfer to a wire rack and let cool slightly. Lightly
dust all over with the confectioners' sugar and cinnamon
mixture. Serve immediately.

. . .

# Little Scallion & Ricotta Tarts

*Simply flavored ricotta and pecorino cheese make a light but tasty filling for these crisp little tarts. They would be perfect as an appetizer or as a delicious light lunch served with a fresh green salad.*

MAKES 12

## Ingredients

### Pastry Dough
1⅓ CUPS ALL-PURPOSE FLOUR,
  PLUS 1 TABLESPOON FOR DUSTING
PINCH OF SALT
1 STICK BUTTER, DICED, PLUS
  ½ TABLESPOON FOR GREASING
1 EGG YOLK

### Filling
1 CUP RICOTTA CHEESE
1 CUP GRATED PECORINO CHEESE
1 EGG, BEATEN
12 SCALLIONS, FINELY CHOPPED
2 TABLESPOONS FRESH SHELLED
  PEAS, LIGHTLY COOKED AND COOLED
1 TEASPOON GREEN PEPPERCORNS IN
  LIQUID, DRAINED
SALT AND PEPPER (OPTIONAL)

1. To make the dough, sift the flour and salt into a bowl or food processor, add the butter, and rub in with your fingertips or process until the mixture resembles fine bread crumbs. Add the egg yolk and enough cold water to form a smooth dough. Cover and chill in the refrigerator for 30 minutes.

2. Preheat the oven to 375°F. Lightly grease a 12-cup muffin pan.

3. Roll out the dough on a floured work surface to a thickness of ½ inch. Using a plain round cutter, cut out circles large enough to line the cups in the muffin pan. Gently press the pastry shells into the cups. Line each pastry shell with a small piece of parchment paper and fill with pie weights or dried beans.

4. Bake the pastry shells in the preheated oven for 4-5 minutes, until golden and crisp. Remove the paper and weights.

5. Meanwhile, to make the filling, mix the ricotta cheese and pecorino cheese together in a large bowl. Add the egg, scallions, and peas. Chop the peppercorns finely, then add to the mixture. Season to taste with salt and pepper, if using.

6. Spoon the filling into the pastry shells and bake for 10 minutes, or until golden. Serve warm.

...

# Kale, Shallot & Blue Cheese Biscuits

*Kale makes a hearty addition to a biscuit mix. Shallots add a little sweetness and moisture, while blue cheese enriches the flavor. Serve freshly baked and lavishly spread with unsalted butter.*

## MAKES 10-12

### Ingredients

8 OUNCES TRIMMED KALE

2 TABLESPOONS VEGETABLE OIL

2 SMALL SHALLOTS,
  FINELY CHOPPED

2 CUPS WHOLE WHEAT FLOUR

2 TEASPOONS SUPERFINE SUGAR

2 TEASPOONS BAKING POWDER

½ TEASPOON BAKING SODA

¼ TEASPOON SALT

¼ TEASPOON PEPPER

4 TABLESPOONS CHILLED
  BUTTER, DICED

1 CUP CRUMBLED BLUE CHEESE

1 EGG, LIGHTLY BEATEN

ABOUT ½ CUP BUTTERMILK

1 TABLESPOON ALL-PURPOSE FLOUR,
  FOR DUSTING

1 EGG YOLK

1 TABLESPOON MILK

UNSALTED BUTTER, TO SERVE
  (OPTIONAL)

---

1. Put the kale into the top of a steamer and steam for 7-10 minutes, until tender. Remove from the heat and let cool. Finely chop, then squeeze with your hands to remove as much liquid as possible.

2. Meanwhile, heat the oil in a small skillet over medium heat. Add the shallots and gently sauté for about 5 minutes, until soft. Remove from the heat and let cool.

3. Preheat the oven to 400°F. Line a baking sheet with a silicone sheet or nonstick parchment paper.

4. Put the flour, sugar, baking powder, baking soda, salt, and pepper into the bowl of a food processor and pulse briefly to mix. Add the butter and pulse a few more times until crumbly. Add the shallots, kale, and ½ cup of the cheese. Pulse again to mix. Pour in the beaten egg and scant ½ cup of the buttermilk. Pulse briefly to a soft, slightly sticky dough. Add a little more buttermilk if the mixture seems dry.

5. Turn out the dough onto a well-floured pastry mat or board. Use a floured rolling pin to lightly roll out the dough to a ¾-inch-thick circle.

6. Using a 2½-inch plain cutter, cut out 10-12 circles, or cut out triangles using a sharp knife. Arrange on the prepared sheet.

7. Mix the egg yolk with the milk and brush over the tops of the biscuits. Sprinkle with the remaining cheese. Bake in the middle of the preheated oven for 15-18 minutes, or until well risen and the tip of a knife inserted into the center of a biscuit comes out clean.

8. Slice the biscuits in half and spread with butter before serving, if using. These are best served freshly baked.

. . .

Cook's Tip

For best results, dip the edge of the cutter into a little oil or flour before cutting out the biscuits. Press down firmly into the dough without twisting.

# Cheese, Chile & Potato Empanadas

Baked in the oven, these meltingly crisp pies are a healthier take on the usual fried version. Chargrilled chiles and nuggets of potato mixed with tangy feta and gooey melted mozzarella make an irresistible filling. Smoky chipotle chile and fresh cilantro perk up the sour cream sauce.

## Cook's Tip

These pies are big, so you will need to bake them in batches. Make sure that you plan in enough baking time.

## Variation

Try replacing the potato for the filling with some cooked and mashed black beans. You could also add a handful of frozen corn kernels.

MAKES 12

## Ingredients

### Dough

3⅓ CUPS ALL-PURPOSE FLOUR
¾ TEASPOON SALT
1½ STICKS CHILLED UNSALTED
  BUTTER, DICED
1 EGG
¼ CUP WATER

### Filling

6 GREEN CHILES (ABOUT 8 OUNCES)
1½ CUPS SHREDDED MOZZARELLA CHEESE
⅔ CUP CRUMBLED FETA CHEESE
½ RED ONION, FINELY CHOPPED
1 TEASPOON DRIED OREGANO

1 TEASPOON CUMIN SEEDS, CRUSHED
¼ TEASPOON SALT
¼ TEASPOON PEPPER
1 RUSSET POTATO, COOKED AND DICED
1 EGG YOLK
1 TABLESPOON MILK

### Sauce

1 CUP SOUR CREAM
JUICE OF ½ LIME
2-3 TABLESPOONS CHILES IN
  ADOBO SAUCE
⅓ CUP CHOPPED FRESH CILANTRO

1. To make the dough, mix the flour and salt in a food processor. Add the butter, egg, and water, and pulse briefly until clumps form. Do not overwork the dough. Shape into a flattened ball and chill in the refrigerator for 30 minutes.

2. To make the filling, put the chiles onto a baking sheet under a hot broiler. Broil for 8-10 minutes, turning once, until the skin is black. Cover with a dish towel and let rest for 10 minutes. Peel off the skin, remove the stem and seeds, and coarsely chop the flesh. Preheat the oven to 425°F. Line a baking sheet with a silicone sheet.

3. Put the chiles, mozzarella cheese, feta cheese, onion, oregano, cumin, salt, and pepper into a bowl and lightly mix with a fork.

4. Put the prepared baking sheet into the preheated oven. Divide the dough into 12 pieces and shape into balls. Flatten slightly, then roll out each ball to a 6-inch circle, neatening the edges with a cookie cutter.

5. Place 2 tablespoons of the cheese mixture and a few pieces of potato in one half of each circle. Moisten the edges with water, fold over, and seal. Crimp the edges with a fork. Mix the egg yolk and milk in a small bowl. Brush over the empanadas. Place on the preheated baking sheet and bake for 15-20 minutes, until golden.

6. Meanwhile, mix the sauce ingredients together in a serving bowl. Serve the empanadas warm or at room temperature with the sauce.

. . .

# Hints and Tips for Vegetable Know-How

Knowing what to look for in terms of quality is just as important as technical skill in the kitchen. After all, you wouldn't dream of choosing second-rate fruit or fish, so why not be discerning with vegetables?

## Freshness Check
*There are a few things you can check to determine the freshness of vegetables.*

COLOR—It should be clear and vibrant. Say no to yellowing greens.
FIRMNESS AND WEIGHT—Vegetables should feel firm and heavy for their size. If they are unexpectedly light, they may be dry inside.
SKIN—Look for taut, undamaged skin. Wrinkled skin is a clear sign of age.
CUT ENDS—These should look fresh and moist with no hint of brown.
SMELL—It should be pleasantly clean instead of rotting or otherwise unpleasant.

## Prepping Vegetables
*Different types of vegetable require different preparation techniques.*

RAW VEGETABLES—Roots with dense flesh or firm cabbage need really fine shredding to produce a light cake with a good crumb. The finest grating disk of a food processor will do this in seconds. For a superfine texture, follow up with the chopping blade.
LEAFY GREENS—Soft, leafy greens, such as spinach or Swiss chard, need cooking, draining, and squeezing. If used raw, they exude moisture and make the mixture too wet.
STARCHY VEGETABLES—To prevent starchy vegetables, such as potatoes and parsnips, from becoming waterlogged, steam them instead of boiling. They can be pureed in a food processor, but be sure to pulse in short bursts, or the starch molecules will combine to produce a gluelike texture. A potato ricer is a good alternative to a food processor.

## Wet or Woody?
*Wet vegetables soften a cake, and woody ones add structure and texture.*

WET: Cucumbers, pumpkins, Swiss chard, zucchini
MEDIUM WET: Bell peppers, broccoli, cauliflower, eggplant, spinach
WOODY: Celeriac, parsnips, peas, yams
MEDIUM WOODY: Beets, carrots, fennel, potatoes, turnips

Wet and medium wet vegetables should be cooked, drained, and squeezed well to remove excess liquid. Alternatively, they can be shredded and spread out on paper towels to drain.

Woody and medium woody vegetables should be finely chopped, shredded, or precooked before being added to your baked goods.

## Culinary Partnerships
*Use other ingredients to enhance the flavor and texture of your baked goods.*
> Chocolate is a great companion for beets.
> Chopped apple, nuts, and candied fruit add interesting crunch to soft vegetables, such as spinach or Swiss chard.
> Cardamom, cinnamon, and ginger work well with parsnips, pumpkins, and sweet potatoes.
> Nutmeg is a perfect partner for cabbage and leafy greens.
> Orange juice and grated orange peel are delicious with carrots.
> Freshly ground black pepper perks up all root vegetables.

## Bakers' Hints and Tips
*There are some handy tricks of the trade that you can employ to be sure of perfect baking results every time.*
> Use a flat, heavy metal baking sheet for cookies.
> For a foolproof nonstick surface, line baking sheets with silicone sheets that can withstand high temperatures.
> Rotate the baking sheet or pan halfway through baking for even browning.
> Let cakes cool completely before frosting or icing. Even a little residual warmth will cause the topping to melt.
> Don't pour heated butter or liquids onto a mixture containing beaten eggs, or you may end up with scrambled eggs.

# CHAPTER 4:

## Pies & Desserts

# Spiced Pumpkin Pie with Pecans

*This rich pie is ideal warm or cold as a dessert for a dinner party or as an afternoon treat. The almond pastry adds a sweet nuttiness.*

SERVES 8

## Ingredients

### Pastry Dough
¾ CUP GROUND ALMONDS
  (ALMOND MEAL)
1½ TABLESPOONS BUTTER, DICED
1 TABLESPOON COCONUT FLOUR
1 TABLESPOON STEVIA
1 EGG
PINCH OF SEA SALT

### Filling
6 CUPS PEELED, SEEDED, AND
  DICED BUTTERNUT SQUASH, OR
  1 (15-OUNCE) CAN PUMPKIN PUREE
  (NOT PUMPKIN PIE FILLING)
2 TABLESPOONS COCONUT FLOUR
2 TABLESPOONS STEVIA
1½ TEASPOONS GROUND CINNAMON
1 TEASPOON FRESHLY GRATED
  NUTMEG
1½ TABLESPOONS BUTTER, DICED
2 EGGS

3 TABLESPOONS HEAVY CREAM
3 TABLESPOONS COARSELY CHOPPED
  PECANS

1. Preheat the oven to 325°F. Line a
9-inch fluted nonstick tart pan with
parchment paper.

2. To make the dough, put all the ingredients
into a food processor and process to a soft
dough. Press it into the prepared pan, pushing
it up the sides. Prick all over with a fork.
Bake in the preheated oven for 15 minutes,
or until golden. Remove from the oven and let
cool. Do not turn off the oven.

3. Meanwhile, make the filling. If using
fresh squash, bring a large saucepan of
water to a boil, add the squash, bring back
to a boil, and cook for 10 minutes, or until
soft. Drain, then let cool. Put the coconut
flour, stevia, cinnamon, nutmeg, and boiled
squash or pumpkin puree in a food processor
and process until smooth. Add the butter,
eggs, and cream and process again. Transfer
the mixture to the tart shell.

4. Sprinkle the nuts over the filling and bake
for 55-60 minutes, or until the sides are set
but the center has a slight wobble.

...

## Cook's Tip

*To make parchment paper really
pliable, screw it up into a ball
before you use it; all the creases
will then fit easily into the
fluted edge of the pan.*

# Parsnip Lemon Meringue with Hazelnut Pastry

*Pureed with lemon juice, unrefined sugar, and fresh eggs, versatile parsnips make a creamy citrus filling that will have your guests guessing. The pleasantly sharp flavor makes a wonderful contrast to the sweet meringue and crunchy nut pastry.*

SERVES 6

## Ingredients

3 PARSNIPS, THINLY SLICED
  INTO CIRCLES
¾ TABLESPOON FINELY GRATED
  LEMON ZEST
JUICE OF 2 LEMONS
¼ CUP GRANULATED SUGAR
2 EGG YOLKS

### Hazelnut Pastry Dough

½ CUP SKINNED HAZELNUTS,
  TOASTED AND COARSELY CHOPPED
1¼ CUPS ALL-PURPOSE FLOUR,
  PLUS 1 TABLESPOON FOR DUSTING

¼ CUP SUPERFINE SUGAR
PINCH OF SALT
6 TABLESPOONS CHILLED
  UNSALTED BUTTER, DICED, PLUS
  ½ TABLESPOON FOR GREASING
2 EGG YOLKS
1-2 TABLESPOONS CHILLED WATER

### Meringue

2 EGG WHITES,
  AT ROOM TEMPERATURE
PINCH OF SALT
½ CUP SUPERFINE SUGAR

---

1. To make the dough, put the hazelnuts into a food processor and grind to a powder. Add the flour, sugar, and salt. Pulse briefly to combine. Add the butter and pulse again until crumbly. Pour in the egg yolks and a little water. Pulse briefly until clumps form. Turn out the dough onto a lightly floured surface and gently mix to a soft dough. Wrap in plastic wrap and chill in the refrigerator for 30 minutes.

2. Meanwhile, put the parsnips into the top of a steamer and steam for 15 minutes, until tender. Let cool slightly, then puree with the lemon zest, lemon juice, granulated sugar, and egg yolks.

3. Preheat the oven to 375°F. Grease a 9½-inch loose-bottom tart pan.

4. Roll out the dough and use it to line the prepared pan. Line with aluminum foil and pie weights or dried beans. Bake in the preheated oven for 10 minutes, then remove the foil and weights. Bake for an additional 5-10 minutes, or until the bottom is crisp. Remove from the oven. Reduce the oven temperature to 325°F. Spoon the parsnip puree into the pastry shell.

5. To make the meringue, put the egg whites into a bowl with the salt and whisk with a handheld electric mixer until they hold soft peaks. Add the sugar, a spoonful at a time, and beat until stiff. Spoon the meringue into the pastry shell and bake for 30-40 minutes, until golden. Let cool in the pan for 10 minutes, then turn out. Serve warm.

. . .

# Sweet Pepper Upside-Down Tart with Black Pepper Caramel

*Coated in a deliciously sticky black pepper glaze, vibrant strips of red bell pepper take on a new dimension in this stunning upside-down dessert. This is a stylish dessert to round off a dinner party.*

## SERVES 8

### Ingredients

1½ STICKS UNSALTED BUTTER,
 PLUS ½ TABLESPOON FOR GREASING
2 SMALL RED BELL PEPPERS,
 SEEDED AND HALVED LENGTHWISE
1⅛ CUPS ALL-PURPOSE FLOUR
2 TEASPOONS BAKING POWDER
½ CUP GROUND ALMONDS
 (ALMOND MEAL)
¾ CUP SUPERFINE SUGAR
3 EGGS, LIGHTLY BEATEN
1 TEASPOON VANILLA EXTRACT

### Caramel

4 TABLESPOONS UNSALTED BUTTER
¼ CUP GRANULATED SUGAR
1 TEASPOON GOOD-QUALITY
 BLACK PEPPERCORNS, CRACKED

1. Preheat the oven to 350°F. Grease a 9½-inch round springform cake pan and place on a baking sheet.

2. Preheat the broiler to hot. Lay the red bell peppers, cut side down, on a baking sheet and place under the broiler. Broil for 10-12 minutes, until blackened. Cover with a clean dish towel for 10 minutes to loosen the skin.

3. Peel the red bell peppers. Slice in half lengthwise and trim the edges straight. Slice diagonally into ½-inch strips. Arrange attractively in the prepared pan, peeled side down.

4. Sift together the flour, baking powder, and ground almonds into a bowl, adding any coarse almond residue left in the sifter.

5. Put the butter and sugar into a large mixing bowl and cream with a handheld electric mixer for 5 minutes, or until pale and fluffy. Gradually add the sifted flour mixture, alternating with the beaten eggs and vanilla extract and beating well between each addition.

6. To make the caramel, heat the butter, sugar, and peppercorns in a small saucepan over medium-high heat. When the sugar has melted, pour the mixture over the red bell peppers. Working quickly, spoon the flour mixture over the top, leveling the surface with a spatula.

7. Bake the tart in the preheated oven for 30-35 minutes, until a knife inserted into the center comes out clean. Let cool in the pan for 10 minutes.

8. Invert the pan onto a serving plate, then unclip and remove the springform. Serve the cake warm or at room temperature.

...

## Cook's Tip

Use a pastry brush to move the bell pepper strips around to let the caramel spread among them.

# Caramelized Fennel & Honey Clafoutis

Thinly sliced and fried with honey until sticky and sweet, licorice-scented fennel is baked in a wholesome mixture of eggs and milk, sweetened with unrefined sugar. An often overlooked vegetable, fennel really comes into its own in this simple dessert.

## Cook's Tip

If the fennel starts to brown, cover the dish with aluminum foil near the end of the cooking time.

**SERVES 5-6**

## Ingredients

3 SMALL FENNEL BULBS
4 TABLESPOONS UNSALTED BUTTER
1 TEASPOON FENNEL SEEDS,
  LIGHTLY CRUSHED
1 TABLESPOON MILD HONEY, SUCH
  AS ACACIA
SQUEEZE OF LEMON JUICE
1 TABLESPOON GRANULATED SUGAR,
  FOR SPRINKLING

## Batter

½ TABLESPOON BUTTER,
  FOR GREASING
3 EGGS, LIGHTLY BEATEN
1¼ CUPS MILK
¼ CUP GRANULATED SUGAR
1 TABLESPOON VANILLA EXTRACT
½ CUP PLUS 1 TABLESPOON
  ALL-PURPOSE FLOUR, SIFTED

*1.* Preheat the oven to 350°F and grease an 8 x 11-inch baking dish.

*2.* To make the batter, whisk together all the ingredients in a bowl and set aside.

*3.* Trim the fennel, discarding the coarse outer layers. Slice the bulbs lengthwise into thin segments.

*4.* Heat the butter in a skillet over medium heat. Add the fennel, fennel seeds, honey, and lemon juice. Gently sauté for about 15 minutes, stirring regularly, until the fennel is golden and sticky.

*5.* Meanwhile, pour a thin film of batter into the bottom of the prepared dish. Bake in the preheated oven for 5-7 minutes, or until just set.

*6.* Arrange the fennel on top of the batter, spooning over any sediment from the pan. Pour the remaining batter over the top.

*7.* Return to the oven and bake for 40-50 minutes, or until puffy and golden and a knife inserted into the center comes out clean.

*8.* Sprinkle with a little sugar and serve warm.

...

# Carrots & Peaches with Pistachio Crumble Topping

## SERVES 6

### Ingredients

4 TABLESPOONS UNSALTED BUTTER,
  PLUS ½ TABLESPOON FOR GREASING
4 RIPE PEACHES
3-4 CARROTS, PEELED
1½ TEASPOONS CUMIN SEEDS,
  LIGHTLY CRUSHED
3 TABLESPOONS GRANULATED SUGAR
THINLY PARED ZEST AND JUICE OF
  1 LARGE ORANGE

### Crumble Topping

1 CUP ROLLED OATS
¾ CUP ALL-PURPOSE FLOUR
1 STICK BUTTER
½ CUP GRANULATED SUGAR
2 TEASPOONS CUMIN SEEDS,
  LIGHTLY CRUSHED
2 TEASPOONS VANILLA EXTRACT
¼ CUP SHELLED PISTACHIO NUTS,
COARSELY CHOPPED

1. Preheat the oven to 375°F. Grease an 8 x 11-inch baking dish. Line a baking sheet with nonstick parchment paper.

2. To make the crumble topping, combine all the ingredients, except the nuts, in the bowl of a food processor. Pulse in short bursts until the mixture starts to clump. Turn out the mixture onto a board.

3. Press the nuts evenly into the topping mixture. Spread the mixture in a ½-inch thick layer on the prepared baking sheet, flattening it with your fingers. Bake in the preheated oven for 15 minutes, or until golden around the edges. Remove from the oven (do not turn off the oven) and let cool and become crisp.

4. Meanwhile, halve the peaches lengthwise and remove the pits. Slice each half into three segments.

5. Cut the carrots into 2-inch sticks. Using a swivel peeler, shave into wafers, rotating each stick as you do so. Discard the woody core.

6. Heat the butter and cumin seeds in a large skillet over medium-high heat. Add the sugar and stir until melted. Add the carrot wafers and sauté for 10 minutes, or until tender. Add the peaches and the orange zest and juice. Cook for 2-3 minutes, until heated through.

7. Transfer the carrots, peaches, and buttery juices to the baking dish. Break the topping into small chunks and arrange on top of the filling. Bake for 15-20 minutes, until bubbling.

8. Serve warm or at room temperature.

...

84

# Parsnip, Pear & Almond Cobbler

**SERVES 5-6**

## Ingredients

4 TABLESPOONS UNSALTED BUTTER,
 PLUS ½ TABLESPOON FOR GREASING
3 PARSNIPS
4 FIRM PEARS, SUCH AS BOSC
JUICE OF 1 LARGE LEMON
SEEDS FROM 5 CARDAMOM PODS,
 LIGHTLY CRUSHED
¼ CUP SUPERFINE SUGAR, PLUS
 1 TABLESPOON FOR SPRINKLING
3 TABLESPOONS SLIVERED ALMONDS

## Pastry Dough

1¼ CUPS ALL-PURPOSE FLOUR
¾ CUP GROUND ALMONDS
 (ALMOND MEAL)
2 TEASPOONS BAKING POWDER
½ CUP SUPERFINE SUGAR
SEEDS FROM 4 CARDAMOM PODS,
 GROUND TO A COARSE POWDER
6 TABLESPOONS CHILLED UNSALTED
 BUTTER, DICED
1 EGG
½ CUP BUTTERMILK

*1.* Preheat the oven to 375°F. Grease a 9 x 12-inch oval baking dish.

*2.* To make the dough, sift together the flour, ground almonds, and baking powder into the bowl of a food processor. Add the sugar and cardamom and pulse briefly to mix. Add the butter and pulse again until the mixture resembles coarse crumbs.

*3.* Lightly beat the egg with the buttermilk. Add to the dry ingredients and lightly pulse until a soft dough forms. Scrape into a bowl and set aside.

*4.* Slice the parsnips into 2 x ½-inch stick shapes. Place in the top of a steamer and steam for 10 minutes, until tender.

*5.* Meanwhile, quarter, core, and peel the pears. Slice each quarter in half lengthwise and put into a bowl with the lemon juice.

*6.* Heat the butter in a large skillet over medium-high heat. Add the crushed cardamom seeds and the sugar. Stir for a few seconds, then add the parsnips, crushing them lightly with the back of a wooden spoon to break them up. Sauté for 2-3 minutes. Add the pears and their juices. cook for 3-5 minutes to heat through.

*7.* Transfer the pear-and-parsnip mixture to the baking dish. Dot with walnut-size dollops of dough and sprinkle with the slivered almonds.

*8.* Bake in the preheated oven for 30-35 minutes, until golden. Sprinkle with the sugar. Serve warm or at room temperature.

# Rhubarb & Orange Crisp

*This family dessert is given a lift with the addition of tangy orange zest and juice. The oats add a wonderful crunchy texture to the crisp topping.*

SERVES 4

## Ingredients

10 RHUBARB STALKS
   (ABOUT 1 POUND), CHOPPED
¼ CUP SUPERFINE SUGAR
FINELY GRATED ZEST AND
   JUICE OF 1 ORANGE

## Crisp Topping

⅓ CUP ALL-PURPOSE FLOUR
¼ CUP FIRMLY PACKED LIGHT
   BROWN SUGAR
4 TABLESPOONS UNSALTED BUTTER
½ CUP ROLLED OATS
⅓ CUP GROUND ALMONDS
   (ALMOND MEAL)

1. Preheat the oven to 400°F. Put the rhubarb, sugar, and orange zest and juice into a saucepan and heat over medium heat until boiling. Reduce the heat, cover, and simmer for about 5 minutes, until the rhubarb is just tender.

2. Transfer to a 1¼-quart ovenproof dish and place on a baking sheet.

3. To make the crisp topping, put the flour and sugar into a bowl and mix together. Add the butter and rub it in with your fingertips until you have a crumbly mixture. Stir in the oats and almonds.

4. Sprinkle the topping evenly over the fruit and bake the dessert in the preheated oven for 25-30 minutes, until golden brown. Serve warm.

...

## Cook's Tip

*This dessert is delicious on its own, but you could add a little touch of luxury by serving it with with vanilla ice cream or frozen yogurt, or by pouring some cream on the side.*

# Peppercorn Meringue Roulade

Crisp but marshmallowy meringue, flecked with crushed green peppercorns, is rolled around a summery filling of cream cheese, marinated cucumber, strawberries, and mint. This is a showstopper of a dessert that will have your guests clamoring for more.

## SERVES 8

### Ingredients

1 LARGE CUCUMBER, QUARTERED
  LENGTHWISE AND SEEDED
2 TABLESPOONS SUPERFINE SUGAR,
  PLUS 1 TABLESPOON FOR
  SPRINKLING
1 CUP CREAM CHEESE
1 CUP HEAVY CREAM
1 TABLESPOON CHOPPED FRESH MINT,
  PLUS A FEW SMALL MINT LEAVES,
  TO DECORATE

2 TEASPOONS DRIED GREEN
  PEPPERCORNS, LIGHTLY CRUSHED
2 CUPS HULLED AND THINLY SLICED
  FRAGRANT STRAWBERRIES, AT ROOM
  TEMPERATURE (SLICED LENGTHWISE)

### Meringue

4 EGG WHITES
PINCH OF SALT
1¼ CUPS SUPERFINE SUGAR
1 TABLESPOON DRIED GREEN
  PEPPERCORNS, LIGHTLY CRUSHED

1. Preheat the oven to 350°F. Line a 13 x 9-inch baking pan
with parchment paper.

2. Thinly slice the cucumber quarters diagonally. Put into a
strainer over a bowl and sprinkle with sugar. Let drain for
at least 1 hour, stirring occasionally.

3. Meanwhile, to make the meringue, put the egg whites into
a large, grease-free bowl. Add the salt and whisk with a
handheld electric mixer for about 3 minutes, until they hold
stiff peaks. Beat in the sugar, 1 tablespoon at a time, then
stir in the peppercorns.

4. Spoon the meringue into the prepared pan and level the
surface. Bake in the preheated oven for 6-8 minutes, until
pale golden. Reduce the oven temperature to 275°F and bake
for an additional 10 minutes.

5. Turn out the meringue onto a sheet of parchment paper.
Peel away the paper lining and let cool for 10 minutes.

6. Beat together the cream cheese, sugar, and cream until
stiff. Add the mint and peppercorns. Spread evenly over the
meringue, leaving a ¾-inch margin at each end.

7. Remove the cucumber from the strainer and thoroughly dry
with paper towels. Sprinkle the cucumber and strawberry
slices evenly over the cream, reserving a few to decorate.

8. Roll up the meringue from the short ends, using the
paper to lift it. Transfer to a serving dish and chill
for 30 minutes. Decorate with the reserved cucumber and
strawberry slices and the mint leaves. Serve immediately.

...

# Beet Roulade with Chocolate, Tangerine & Cherry Filling

Beets add moistness and color to this virtually fat-free whisked cake roll. A delectable filling of cream cheese and white chocolate is sharpened with grated tangerine peel and simply delicious dried cherries. Perfect for a stylish afternoon snack.

## SERVES 8-10

### Ingredients

4 BEETS, SLICED
1 TABLESPOON OIL, FOR OILING
1⅓ CUPS ALL-PURPOSE FLOUR,
  PLUS 1 TABLESPOON FOR DUSTING
2 TABLESPOONS UNSWEETENED
  COCOA POWDER
1 TEASPOON BAKING SODA
4 EGGS
1 CUP SUPERFINE SUGAR,
  PLUS 1 TABLESPOON FOR DUSTING
2 TEASPOONS VANILLA EXTRACT
½ CUP BUTTERMILK

### Filling

2½ OUNCES WHITE CHOCOLATE
⅔ CUP CREAM CHEESE
4 TABLESPOONS UNSALTED BUTTER,
  AT ROOM TEMPERATURE
⅓ CUP CONFECTIONERS' SUGAR,
  SIFTED, PLUS 1 TABLESPOON
  FOR DUSTING
½ TEASPOON VANILLA EXTRACT
FINELY GRATED ZEST OF
  1 TANGERINE
½ CUP DRIED CHERRIES

---

*1.* Put the beets into the top of a steamer and steam for
30 minutes, then puree in a blender until smooth. Transfer
to a bowl and set aside until needed.

*2.* Preheat the oven to 375°F. Oil a 14 x 10-inch baking pan
and line with parchment paper. Dust with flour, tipping out
any excess. Sift the flour, cocoa powder, and baking soda
twice into a bowl. Beat the eggs and sugar with a handheld
electric mixer for 6-8 minutes, until thick and creamy. Beat
in the beet puree and vanilla extract. Gradually beat in the
flour mixture, alternating with the buttermilk.

*3.* Pour the batter into the prepared pan and bake in the
preheated oven for 10-15 minutes, or until the top springs
back when lightly pressed. Lightly dust a sheet of wax paper
with superfine sugar. Turn out the cake onto the prepared
paper. Peel off the parchment paper, then roll up the cake
from the narrow end, with the wax paper inside. Let cool.

*4.* To make the filling, put the chocolate into a heatproof bowl
set over a saucepan of gently simmering water and heat until
melted. Let cool slightly, then mix with the cheese, butter,
confectioners' sugar, vanilla extract, and tangerine zest.

*5.* Carefully unroll the cake and remove the paper. Spread
the filling evenly over the surface. Sprinkle with the
cherries, roll up, wrap tightly in plastic wrap, and chill
for at least 1 hour. Place the roulade on a serving plate,
seam side down. Remove a thin slice from each end for a neat
appearance, then dust with the confectioners' sugar. Cut
into slices to serve.

...

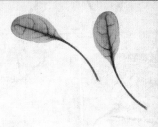

# Swiss Chard & Ricotta Phyllo Pie

*Swiss chard adds an earthier flavor than the spinach typically used in this layered pie. The pine nuts provide great texture and crunch and the Parmesan cheese brings a sharp note to the creamy ricotta.*

## SERVES 9

### Ingredients

2 POUNDS RAINBOW SWISS CHARD
4 TABLESPOONS BUTTER, PLUS
½ TABLESPOON FOR GREASING
2 LEEKS, SLICED
2 GARLIC CLOVES, THINLY SLICED
3 TABLESPOONS CHOPPED MIXED
FRESH HERBS, SUCH AS THYME,
MARJORAM, AND FLAT-LEAF
PARSLEY
1¾ CUPS RICOTTA CHEESE

½ CUP FRESHLY GRATED
PARMESAN CHEESE
⅛ TEASPOON FRESHLY GRATED
NUTMEG
2 EGGS, BEATEN
12 LARGE SHEETS PHYLLO PASTRY
1 TABLESPOON OLIVE OIL,
FOR BRUSHING
⅓ CUP PINE NUTS
SEA SALT AND PEPPER (OPTIONAL)

1. Chop the Swiss chard stems into chunks. Slice the leaves into thin ribbons.

2. Heat the butter in a large skillet over medium heat. Add the leeks and Swiss chard stems, then cover and sauté for 5-7 minutes, until soft.

3. Add the Swiss chard leaves, garlic, and herbs. Cover and gently sauté until the leaves are tender. Transfer the vegetables to a colander and drain.

4. Beat together the ricotta cheese, Parmesan cheese, nutmeg, and eggs in a large bowl. Mix in the drained vegetables. Season with salt and pepper, if using.

5. Preheat the oven to 375°F and grease a 9 x 12-inch baking pan. Place a sheet of pastry in the prepared pan, trimming to fit as necessary. Brush with oil and sprinkle with a few pine nuts. Add another five sheets, lightly brushing each one with oil and sprinkling with pine nuts.

6. Pour in the filling and level the surface. Cover with another five sheets of phyllo pastry, brushing each sheet with oil and sprinkling with pine nuts. Add the final sheet and brush with oil.

7. Using a sharp knife, cut through all the pastry and filling layers to make 3-inch squares.

8. Bake the pie in the preheated oven for 35-40 minutes, until golden and crisp. Serve hot or at room temperature.

...

## Cook's Tip

*Grana Padano cheese would make an economical alternative to the Parmesan, and will work well in this recipe.*

# Caramelized Rutabaga & Ham Pie

*This hearty winter pie would make a substantial lunch dish, or you could serve it as a main dish with mashed potatoes and cooked peas, green beans, or steamed spinach.*

## SERVES 4

### Ingredients

1¼ POUNDS COOKED HAM,
CUT INTO CUBES

6 TABLESPOONS BUTTER

2 ONIONS, CHOPPED

3 CUPS DICED RUTABAGA OR
SWEET POTATOES

1 TEASPOON CHOPPED
FRESH SAGE

3 TABLESPOONS ALL-PURPOSE
FLOUR, PLUS 1 TABLESPOON
FOR DUSTING

2½ CUPS MILK

1 SHEET PREPARED PUFF PASTRY,
THAWED IF FROZEN

1 EGG, BEATEN, FOR BRUSHING

SALT AND PEPPER (OPTIONAL)

---

1. Put the ham into a large bowl and set aside. Melt 4 tablespoons of the butter in a large skillet over medium heat. Add the onions, rutabaga or sweet potato, and sage and season to taste with salt and pepper, if using. Stir well and cook over medium-high heat for 35-40 minutes, occasionally turning over the pieces with a spatula, until golden brown.

2. Meanwhile, melt the remaining butter in a small saucepan over medium heat. Add the flour and cook, stirring, for 1-2 minutes. Gradually add the milk, stirring to make a smooth sauce. Remove from the heat and season with salt and pepper, if using.

3. Preheat the oven to 425°F. Roll out the pastry on a lightly floured surface to a rectangle slightly larger than a 10½ x 7-inch pie plate.

4. When the vegetables are caramelized, add them to the bowl with the ham, then add the white sauce, stirring gently to combine. Transfer the mixture to a pie plate, brush the rim with the beaten egg, and then lay the pastry over the filling.

5. Press the pastry to the rim, then trim off the excess and cut out shapes to decorate the top, if desired. Brush the pastry with the beaten egg and cook in the oven for 15-20 minutes, or until the pastry is puffed and golden. Serve immediately.

. . .

## Cook's Tip

*Cover the dish with aluminum foil toward the end of the cooking time if the pastry begins to brown too quickly.*